PORTRAIT OF
WEST YORKSHIRE

By the same author
Lakeland Discovered

Portrait of
WEST YORKSHIRE

by

Margaret Slack

ROBERT HALE · LONDON

To Geoffrey Whiteley, who loves the hills and valleys

© Margaret Slack 1984
First published in Great Britain 1984

ISBN 0 7090 1550 X

Robert Hale Limited
Clerkenwell House
Clerkenwell Green
London EC1R 0HT

Photoset by Rowland Phototypesetting, Bury St Edmunds, Suffolk.
Printed in Great Britain by St Edmundsbury Press
Bury St Edmunds, Suffolk.
Bound by Woolnough Bookbinding Limited.

CONTENTS

ILLUSTRATIONS

Between pages 160 and 161
Oakwell Hall, Birstall
Nostell Priory
The Holme Valley from Holme
Hebden Bridge
Sowerby Bridge and the Ryburn Valley
Shibden Dale
Stoodley Pike
A view of Halifax from Stoodley Pike
Holme
Moorland at Shipley Glen
The tramway to Shipley Glen
Keighley and Worth Valley train arrives at
   Damens station
Lumb Bridge, a packhorse bridge
The Leeds and Liverpool Canal between Silsden
   and Kildwick
The five rise locks at Bingley
Sunday morning sailing at Wintersett reservoir

All photographs have been taken by the author, apart from that of Waltroyd, which was taken by Jo Kelly; and that of the Tyrls, and the Law Courts, Bradford and the Library, Pontefract, which was taken by Derek G Widdicombe

ACKNOWLEDGEMENTS

The thanks of the author are due to the following: Mr J. B. Nattriss, Reference Librarian, Leeds City Libraries, and his staff; Joyce Hemingway and Joyce Hennessey; Sister Joseph SND; J. B. Priestley and William Heinemann Ltd, for permission to reproduce the extract from *Bright Day*; T. Werner Laurie at the Bodley Head for permission to reproduce the extract 'Un-Satanic Mills' by Wilfred Pickles; Jo Kelly for permission to use the photograph of Waltroyd.

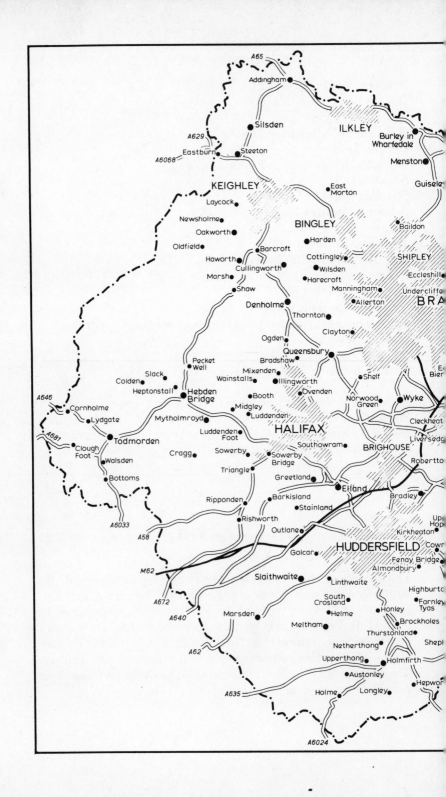

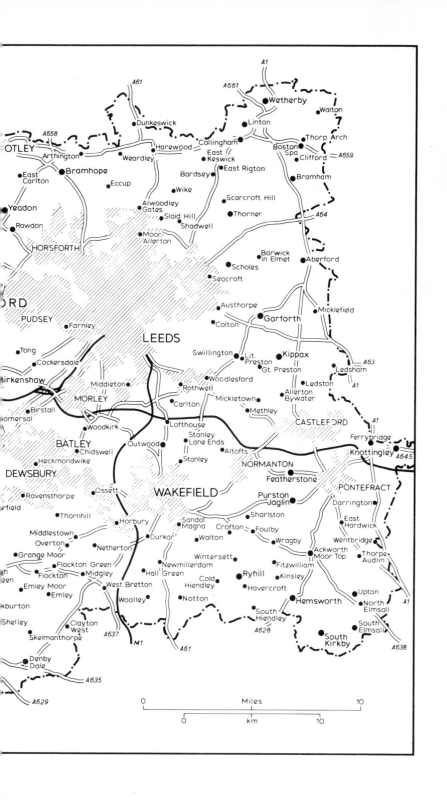

1

The Birth and Death of the West Riding

On 1 April 1974 occurred the biggest shake-up in local government for centuries; probably the biggest in English history.
Traditional boundaries were swept away and new counties were
created; counties were amalgamated, new names were used and
old ones revived. Yorkshire's three Ridings were dismantled
as administrative units, and bits of them handed out elsewhere.

The new order created from the old was carried out with
greater precision, more planning and less bloodshed than when
the old system had been established more than a thousand years
previously.

For some time before the Norman Conquest, England had
consisted of large kingdoms; Deira, an area approximating to
Yorkshire, was part of a larger kingdom of Northumbria. In 867
the Danes, who had invaded parts of England and had settled in
East Anglia, flocked north and captured York, plundering and
pillaging the surrounding country. For the next few years,
although they seem to have left the administration of the
countryside to the Saxons, they remained in York. Gradually,
however, their influence spread and by 876 Deira was so firmly
under Danish control that Healfdene, the Danish chief, was able
to portion out the territory among his followers, and it is
probable that this was the beginning of the three Ridings, East,
North and West. Of these the West Riding was the largest in
terms of area; in fact it was the largest of the English counties,
having 1,776,064 acres; Lincolnshire, the next largest, having
1,705,293 acres. The general trend of the county was north-west
to south-east, and a line from one extremity to the other, i.e.

from Sedbergh in the extreme north-west to Bawtry in the south-west, would measure 93 miles.

Across this area an imaginary line drawn from Saddleworth in the south-west tip to Nun Monkton near York would have measured about 48½ miles. On the north and north-east it was bordered by Westmorland and the North Riding, on the east and south-east by the East Riding, Lincolnshire and Nottinghamshire, on the south-west by Cheshire and Derbyshire and on the west by Lancashire and Westmorland. In many places natural boundaries were used, the rivers Hodder and Ribble in the west, the Derwent in the south-west, the Ure in the north and the Ouse in the east. Alone out of the three Ridings the West Riding had no sea coast.

Topographically and scenically the West Riding was one of the most diverse counties. In the far north-west the wild moors and fells north of Ribblehead and bordering the Dee valley had much more in common with Westmorland than with the West Riding. Further south is a belt of Carboniferous Limestone which is an area of green pastureland with short, springy turf across which white dry-stone walls zigzag irregularly. It is hilly land, and masses of scree formed by weathering have slithered to the bottom of the hills, making one want to go round with a brush and dustpan and sweep them up. The block of limestone thrown up between the North and Mid Craven Faults contains some of the most spectacular scenery in the north of England. The limestone is pure, free from bands of shale or sandstones, and appears very white. Three of its most remarkable features are Malham Cove, a great inland cliff with a black mark down the front where Water Baby Tom is supposed to have slid, Smearsett Scar, a snout-like hump near Stainforth, which viewed from the front would pass for a scene from the Dolomites, and further east the bulge of Kilnsey Crag overlooking the road.

Characteristic of this scar limestone are the clints, or large blocks of limestone separated by grikes, or narrow fissures, formed by weathering. These, in extent, form limestone pavements such as those on top of Malham Cove and on the lower slopes of Ingleborough. This is the country of Yorkshire's highest mountains, the three peaks of Whernside, Ingleborough and Penyghent, the last named having distinct shapes. A vast subterranean world exists in this area, surface water on the Millstone Grit disappearing underground on meeting the limestone belt, creating over millions of years a whole world of caves and pot-holes and tortuous passages. Notable among these are Gaping Gill on the slopes of Ingleborough, the enormous and impressive Hull Pot and the sinister slit of Hunt Pot like a giant's letter box, both on the slopes of Penyghent.

To the south of this limestone region lies an area of Millstone Grit merging into coal measures. Much of the land is heather moor and upland pasture, and there are wide, level moors with broad areas of peat bog. In places the Gritstone forms bold and steep escarpments, typical being that forming the watershed between the Aire and the Wharfe, of which Otley Chevin is part. This area was the manufacturing part of the West Riding and is thickly populated with cities, towns and villages and with houses and mills blackened by a century of grime. But it is also a region of rolling hills with green fields neatly patchworked by black walls and abundant woodland, having a greater topographical affinity with the Lancashire valleys than with the flatter area of coal measures to the south.

West Yorkshire is a truncated version of the West Riding. The River Wharfe forms the northern boundary and at its eastern end turns sharply south not far beyond Wetherby and roughly follows the A1 as far south as South Elmsall. In the west the boundary turns south just beyond Addingham and includes Kildwick and Keighley, where it follows a route roughly along the Pennine watershed to include Todmorden. The southern boundary is just south of Holmfirth, turning north to include Clayton West and Horbury. The county is drained from west to east by the Wharfe, the Aire and the Calder and south to north by the Colne and the Holme. The north-western section of the old West Riding has been put into Cumbria, where physically and geographically it should have been in the first place. The scar limestone area and the mountains have been given to North Yorkshire while the western agricultural area, the Trough of Bowland and the mixed agricultural/industrial area round Barnoldswick and Earby have been put into Lancashire along with Saddleworth in the south-west.

The change was not achieved without bitterness and rancour.

Barnoldswick and Earby resented being delivered into the hands of the traditional enemy Lancashire. In Cowling a firm and successful stand was made against any merger with the red rose. 'And when Cowling fowk mak up ther minds, nowt'll shift 'em.' Cowling was put into North Yorkshire.

The West Riding was at one time divided into Wapentakes, the traditional weapon-shaking places of the Middle Ages, where there were periodic inspections of weapons which all men were supposed to provide for the defence of the locality.

It was not until nearly the end of the nineteenth century that County Councils and County Borough Councils were set up. Six years later, in 1894, Urban Districts and Rural Districts were formed. In that part of the West Riding which now forms West Yorkshire there were six County Boroughs, ten Boroughs, twenty-nine Urban Districts, two complete Rural Districts and parts of six other Rural Districts. These were swept away in April 1974 and five Metropolitan Boroughs were created, Bradford, Calderdale, with its headquarters at Halifax, Kirklees, with its headquarters at Huddersfield, Leeds and Wakefield.

In four of these areas the pre-eminence of one large town meant that there was no question as to which town should be the seat of government. In Kirklees, however, there were two towns, Dewsbury and Huddersfield, which before 1974 had been County Boroughs. The fact that Huddersfield became the administrative centre of Kirklees has created bitterness in Dewsbury, where people in any case resented being linked with Huddersfield and not Wakefield. Todmorden people, at the far end of Calderdale, feel neglected and unconsidered, referring to Halifax as 'that place at the end of the road'. One woman forgot county pride so far as to suggest that, 'they should have put us in with Lancashire.' Resentment was felt in Leeds when Wakefield, the headquarters of the old West Riding, remained the seat of county government.

The new county of West Yorkshire has an area of 787.29 square miles and a population of 2,021,707. The population of the constituent metropolitan authorities is as follows: Bradford, 454,198; Calderdale, 190,330; Kirklees, 370,579; Leeds, 696,714; Wakefield, 309,886.

2

The Middle Ages

Almost two centuries after the birth of the Ridings came the last invasion of England, one which was to have far-reaching consequences and whose date, 1066, is now perhaps the most widely known in English history. The events preceding William's landing, the preparations and the details of the invasion itself contain the ingredients of drama.

Accustomed as we now are to a monarchy which never dies – 'the king is dead, long live the king' – and to a system in which the reins of power pass painlessly from a king to his successor, we tend to forget that it was not always thus. Before the Norman Conquest it was the assembly of wise men, the Witan, who chose the king. Either that or the contenders fought it out. Edward the Confessor, himself half Norman, had, it is thought, promised the crown to William, Duke of Normandy, or at least promised him the right to present himself to the Witan for election. The pious Edward devoted himself more and more to building churches, to prayer and collecting relics. Increasingly he tended to leave government and administration to Harold Godwinson, who fulfilled the duties of Prime Minister even though the term had not then been coined.

The implications of this were not lost on William. When Harold, as a result of a shipwreck off the coast of Normandy, was fortuitously delivered into his hands, William exacted from him as a price of his ransom a solemn oath, taken on the bones of a saint, that Harold would support him as a candidate for the English throne. This picturesque and bizarre story may or may not be true. Neither may the fact that Edward, on his death bed, named Harold Godwinson as his successor. What is undeniably true was William's wrath upon hearing of Harold's succession to the crown, news of which was brought to him when he was out hunting. He returned to his palace speechless with rage and with characteristic zest and vigour set about raising support, both practical and moral, for his projected invasion of England.

The Saxons did not willingly accept him as king, and it was some considerable time before he gained mastery over all his subjects. His efforts to avenge the slaughter of his garrison in York were ruthless and bloody. His hordes devastated much of the countryside, and among entries in Domesday Book recording ploughland, pastureland, woodland and mills, many manors were recorded as waste. The population fled; where, or for how long, the manors remained depopulated is a matter for conjecture.

William, in accordance it is supposed with promises made when he was gathering support for his invasion, rewarded his followers with grants of land. Since he feared that they might become heady with the grandiose ideas which had impelled him to invade England, he took the precaution, among others, of dispersing their holdings of land throughout the length and breadth of England. In order to see that manors had passed from Saxon to Norman as he had ordained, to ascertain how much geld every manor should pay and to make a register of all land, William compiled Domesday Book.

The Norman hold on the country was tightened even more by building castles – along the coast where the fleets of would-be invaders could easily be spotted and also at strategic points throughout England to quell any incipient revolt, as well as to keep an eye on the surrounding countryside. These castles would not in the first instance have been built of stone: wooden structures were erected in the early years following the Conquest, afterwards to be replaced, perhaps as long as nearly two centuries later, by stone buildings.

One of the largest landholders in Yorkshire was Ilbert de Laci, whose family had come from France at the time of the Conquest. Ilbert, in return for his support, received the gift of 150 manors 'or the greatest part of so many' in the West of Yorkshire, ten in Nottinghamshire and four in Lincolnshire. Pontefract was by far the biggest and most important place which Ilbert received, and it is not difficult to see why he made it the head of his fee. There is, however, some doubt as to whether he in fact built the castle. Pontefract was a borough in the time of the Saxons, and the foundation of the castle is thought by some to date to the Saxon and by others to the Norman period. In the chartulary of Kirkstall Abbey, the castle is said to have been built by Ilbert de Laci but other sources claim that at the time the area was given to de Laci the castle must already have been a fortress of some strength. The matter seems of minor importance; what is significant is that there was a castle at Pontefract in Norman times. Either it was built by the Normans or else they maintained and improved a castle which was already in existence when they arrived.

The site was of strategic value, and an early nineteenth-century history describes an extensive view, claiming that the site was bounded only by the hills of Craven and that the towers of York Minster could be seen. To the east it was possible to follow the course of the River Aire as it flowed towards the Humber, while in a south-east direction one could see land in Nottinghamshire and Lincolnshire. In a south and south-westerly direction it was possible to see the Derbyshire hills.

The castle, at one end of the town, is easily accessible from the main shopping centre. One approaches it at street level, although the bailey is situated on the top of a rocky promontory which would make the fortress, if not impregnable, certainly very difficult to scale from the plain, now a busy main road below. The bailey wall is fringed by trees, and beyond there are the trappings of modernity – the Prince of Wales Colliery on the one hand, housing estates and cooling-towers on another – which detract from the extensiveness of the view. There is little there now to remind us of the former size and glory of Pontefract Castle. The comment of a nineteenth-century traveller is still apt: 'What remains of the once magnificent castle is a mass almost unintelligible.'[1] There is a round tower, almost certainly Norman, and crumbling walls surrounding a green sward. Extensive archaeological work, currently in progress, is being undertaken with a view to increasing the tourist attraction.

Another adventurer who came with William, Duke of Normandy, was William de Warene, who received as a reward for his services 300 manors situated in twelve counties, 139 of them in Norfolk and a great number in Sussex, while in Yorkshire he was granted the lordship of Conisborough. There was already a strongly fortified *burh* at Sandal, near Wakefield, and William de Warene made this the head of his manor. The early buildings were of timber; it was not until nearly a couple of centuries had elapsed that these were replaced by stone. Castles were built primarily as a means of defence but they were also residences, although the barons who owned them moved from manor to manor, and even the most well appointed must have been draughty and uncomfortable; but as the Countess of Warene was an occasional visitor, we may suppose that Sandal was relatively comfortable. In the absence of the family, castles had caretakers; at Sandal money was allowed for the support of the constable, watchman and porter. There were, too, other staff; in 1322 the custodian was paid 2s. a day and his page 12d., while several armed men were each paid 2d. The cooper received 2½d. and his boy 1½d., the janitor 2d., the forester 4d. and his boy 1½d.

The circular stone keep at Sandal had an internal diameter of fifty-five feet, and its walls were fourteen feet thick. A medieval castle needed to be able to house and maintain a garrison of soldiers and, if necessary, withstand siege for several weeks. It was usual to find within the bailey wall a granary, vegetable garden, orchard, poultry run, armoury and blacksmith's shop, and stables for horses as well as quarters for the troops. There was, at Sandal, a deer-park of thirty acres, a garden and a small fishpond – valueless – perhaps the castle sewage was poured into it. Among the goods and chattels were twenty-one cart-horses, forty-six colts, two bulls, twenty-five cows, forty oxen, fourteen pigs, thirty ewes and lambs and 5½ tuns of wine, grain and peas.

Both Pontefract and Sandal suffered siege in the Civil War and along with other inland castles were, in 1646, rendered untenable, since which time they have fallen into decay. Of Sandal there is even less remaining than Pontefract. Standing in the midst of a modern housing estate, the castle is easily accessible to the traveller. There is a double motte which is well defined with small projections of masonry sticking up like decayed teeth. The line of the moat is well defined, and round the whole is a gravel path with seats so that one can admire the splendid view.

Other West Yorkshire castles, at Rothwell and Almondbury, for example, have long since disappeared; the present monument at Almondbury on Castle Hill is a Victorian Diamond Jubilee Tower. Practically all the physical evidence which remains to remind us of the Conquest and the Norman adventurers are the names. There is a De Lacy Lane in Kirkstall, Leeds, and a public house called the 'De Lacy' on Tong Street, Bradford – the spelling is a variable factor; while Rombalds Moor, which forms the watershed between the Aire and the Wharfe, is a corruption of the name de Romillé.

The plethora of church and cathedral building which followed the Conquest sprang less from motives of holy piety than a desire to expiate sin and use some of the money which had accrued as spoils of war. Of this church building there is now scant evidence in West Yorkshire but what does remain is a perfectly proportioned Norman church on the outskirts of Leeds. It serves a residential parish consisting almost wholly of modern houses in a rural setting with gently rolling arable land beyond, the fields bordered by hedges and fences. There was a church at Adel before the present one, built during Saxon times and probably existing until well after the Norman Conquest. This building must have been destroyed to make way for the present church, which was built between 1160 and 1170. This was the period in which Norman architecture had reached the peak of perfection, a fact which is reflected in the excellence of the stonework and masonry at Adel.

The plan of the church is simple: there is a rectangular chancel divided by an arch from a wider rectangular nave which has no aisles. The most impressive feature of the exterior is the south doorway framed in an arch of four orders, each of which shows moulding characteristic of the Norman style of architecture. The outer order and the second have zigzag or chevron markings; the innermost is carved with beaked heads, and the third is moulded with two rolls. There is a pointed gable on whose apex is carved the Agnus Dei, the symbol of John the Baptist; beneath this are five panels of sculpture which represent Our Lord seated in majesty, flanked by four beasts – those of the vision of Ezekiel which are symbolic of the four Evangelists. There is also ornamental carving. The doorway has suffered from the weather and was at one time covered by an unsightly porch which was removed about 1816. It is now covered by a porch to protect it from the elements, and although this is by no means unsightly, it does detract rather from the beauty of the doorway. On the door is a bronze sanctuary handle which consists of a circular plaque on which is the head of a beast shown devouring a human head. Through the mouth is a movable ring. Like the doorway the chancel arch shows rich carving. One of the capitals has a representation of the Baptism of Our Lord by St John the Baptist in Jordan, another a centaur fighting with a lion and gnawed behind by a dragon. On one of the capitals on the south side is a carving of the Crucifixion, and another shows a warrior in full armour.

West Yorkshire was, in the Middle Ages, well supplied with monasteries. The history of medieval monasticism seems to have run in cycles: formation of an Order committed to strict rules of austerity, gradual movement towards greater laxity and worldliness, revivification of monastic life by the formation of a new Order committed afresh to the monastic ideals.

The founding, in the sixth century, of the Benedictine Order was a turning-point in the history of monasticism. Those who joined the Order lived a meagre sort of life, having one meal a day and very seldom eating meat, in fact a diet very similar to that of an Italian peasant of the sixth century. It was a well-ordered life devoted to prayer and manual work in the fields, which, in spite of, or perhaps because of, its rigours, attracted men in increasing numbers, so that by the beginning of the seventh century Benedictine monasticism began to be known outside Italy. By the tenth century the monks were beginning to forget their high-minded vows; laxness and worldliness were gradually taking hold.

In order to bring back monasticism to the ideals of St Benedict, the Cluniac Order was founded in 910. In time too, the Cluniac Order became lax and worldly and itself needed reform, so in 1084 the Carthusian Order was formed and in 1098 the Cistercian Order. These were monastic Orders which followed the Rule of St Benedict, but there were other Orders, not based on the Benedictine Rule, of whom the Augustinians were perhaps the best known. Strictly speaking they were not monks but canons.

There was a Cluniac priory at Pontefract which was founded in 1090 by Robert de Laci, Ilbert's son. The buildings were destroyed in the anarchy but the priory was later rebuilt; and there was also a priory at Arthington for Cluniac nuns. The Augustinian canons established themselves at Nostell Priory, and at Kirklees there was a Cistercian nunnery founded during the reign of Henry II. The Crusading Orders too had property in the county, the Knights Templars, for instance, at Temple Newsam. The properties of the Knights Hospitallers of St John can be recognized by the sign of the double cross, an example of which can still be seen on a house at Greenhill, Bingley.

The major Cistercian foundations in Yorkshire are in North Yorkshire – Fountains, Rievaulx, Byland and Jervaulx, along with the Augustinian priory at Bolton and the Benedictine abbey at Selby. Only one of the major abbeys is in West Yorkshire: the Cistercian monastery at Kirkstall on the outskirts of Leeds. This abbey, now ruined, stands between a busy main road and a railway, but, surprisingly enough, with the roar of traffic to one side and the rattle of trains on the other, the abbey and its grounds are an oasis of peace. There could hardly be a busier spot, and this in itself is an irony, as when the Cistercians founded their houses, they deliberately sought out lonely, desolate and sometimes wild places.

The story of the abbey's foundation is interesting. Henry de Laci, the grandson of that Ilbert de Laci who came over with the Conqueror, fell ill, vowing, if he should recover, to build a monastery in honour of the Holy Virgin. As his health improved, he fulfilled his vow by sending for the Abbot of Fountains Abbey and giving him land at Barnoldswick with sufficient money to found an abbey. In May 1147 Alexander, who was Prior at Fountains, went with twelve monks and ten lay brothers to Barnoldswick to found the abbey. This number was significant, the Prior representing Christ and the twelve monks the Apostles.

Unfortunately Barnoldswick did not turn out to be the haven

of peace and tranquillity that the monks had supposed. They were disturbed by the bells of the parish church and eventually became so irritated and angered by this that, acting in a high-handed and distinctly uncharitable manner, they pulled it down. The rector, understandably, was annoyed and took them to court. It is to the credit of the monks that they were instrumental in getting two churches built to replace the one they had destroyed, but it was obvious that they could no longer stay at Barnoldswick. Were the troubles with the bells not enough, further disasters beset them – it seemed almost like a punishment: robbers stole their property, and a plague of rains, lasting nearly a year, ruined their crops.

On one of his visits to Airedale, Abbot Alexander met a group of brethren who were led by a man named Seleth, who it appeared, had been instructed in a dream to go to a place called Kirkstall. This seemed from his description to be just the place Alexander was looking for as a new home for his monks, and in what appears to have been a 'take-over bid' he persuaded Seleth to let him acquire the site. Some of Seleth's brothers joined Alexander; the others were paid off and moved elsewhere.

Abbot Alexander arranged with Henry de Laci to move his community to Kirkstall, and the foundation date of the new abbey there was 19 May 1152. The abbey was dissolved by Henry VIII in the sixteenth century and fell into disuse and decay. Its ruins have been preserved as an ancient monument, and its extensive grounds make a pleasant place for picnics and outings in the summer months.

There are enough of the abbey ruins to enable one to have a fair idea of the life of the monks in the Middle Ages. The roofless shell of the church is sufficiently complete to convey the austerity which was central to the Cistercian ideal, for they believed in plain, unadorned churches. The west front with its splendid Norman doorway is otherwise gaunt and severe. The Cistercians believed in a life of prayer but also in manual work, and admitted lay brothers to their ranks. These lay brothers were monks, not servants, and, since they could not read, they learnt their services by heart, the reason being that by the time of St Bernard monasticism was a profession of the upper or middle classes, and it was not considered possible to teach the poorer peasants Latin. The lay brethren performed agricultural service although they did say some prayers.

The cloisters can be seen next to the church. While the monastery was functioning, they were used as the monks' workplace; they were covered and it was in their stone seats that the monks sat reading and meditating, studying, copying and illuminating manuscripts. Although the roofing protected them from the worst of the elements – there was of course no heating – it must have been cold and draughty in the winter months. In the summer it was no doubt pleasant sitting in the north cloister protected by the church wall from any wind with the sun shining across the garth. Adjoining the cloister was the library. A decree of 1070 stated that on the Monday following the first Sunday in Lent the monks were to meet in the Chapter House in order to return the book which they had had from the library for a year and obtain a new one. Reading one book a year does not seem very onerous until one remembers that the books were very large and in manuscript, and that reading in the monastic context meant studying and meditating upon the words in the book.

Each day the monks assembled in the Chapter House there to hear read aloud a chapter from the Rule of St Benedict, which was read through completely three times a year. In the Chapter House the abbot dealt with the day-to-day administrative affairs of the monastery; if the day was a saint's day, the saint would be remembered in prayers, and any monk who had neglected his duty would be reprimanded by the abbot.

Unlike some Orders, the Cistercians had no vow of silence although they were not expected to talk. Some speech was necessary from time to time, and this took place in the parlour. South of the parlour a passage led to the infirmary – used for looking after the sick and infirm and also for the very old monks. Routine to the life of most people in the Middle Ages was blood-letting, and the monks were no exception. It was, at best, a weakening operation, and after it the monks were cosseted; they no doubt enjoyed a few days in the infirmary where the rigours of normal life were eased – the food would be better, the rule of silence relaxed, and there would be a fire.

The Benedictine Rule was suitable for Mediterranean climes

but it must have been harsh in the winters of northern Europe. There were few fires at Kirkstall. One was in the infirmary, and obviously one was necessary in the kitchen. The only other fire was that in the warming-house, which was lit between November and March, and it was here that the monks were allowed to come and warm their hands for a minute or two.

Medieval life did not consist entirely of prayer and warfare; there was also trade and industry, the monks themselves being farmers, industrialists and innovators. Situated in wild, desolate country, much of the area near the Cistercian monasteries was eminently suitable for sheep-rearing. It was customary for people to give land to the monasteries in return for prayers for their soul; this was a sort of insurance policy for the Hereafter.

Over the centuries the monasteries acquired hundreds of acres of land; sheep-rearing and a subsequent trade in wool became big business for the – particularly Cistercian – monks. Not all of the land was near to the mother house, and granges were built so that monks could tend the sheep. The clip from the sheep on the land belonging to Kirkstall Abbey was considerable and, even allowing for the fact that the Crown took its cut as tax and so did the Vatican, the income from the wool clip was large. In 1315 best-quality wool was worth 20 marks, medium quality 10½ marks and poorest quality 9½ marks; the amount of the clip was 25 sacks, and the amount in a sack was 364 pounds. As a mark was worth 13s. 4d. the value of first-quality wool was about 9d. a pound, and 9d. was the weekly wage of a labourer.

Monasteries employed tradesmen, as did castles, and for this reason, among others, towns tended to grow round the focal points of a castle or a monastery. It is true that the monks themselves had vowed to live in poverty, but the standard of equipment in the monastery itself was usually of high quality. The forging of iron was carried out by the monks of Kirkstall, and there is also evidence of a foundry there. The Kirkstall trades also included coppersmithing, leadworking, coal-mining, pottery and leatherwork. The Kirkstall monks had land and a forge at Ardsley and also near Seacroft, as well as a coal mine near Cookridge. Monks from the other monasteries in Yorkshire practised industry in the Middle Ages: the monks of Fountains had forges soon after the middle of the twelfth century if not before. At Bradley near Almondbury they were granted all the dead wood they needed for smelting and for charcoal and whatever iron ore they could find. The Rievaulx monks were granted the exclusive mining and smelting rights with sufficient wood for fuel in Shipley, Heaton, Chellow Grange and Harden Wood. They were also given leave to take all the ore they might find in Shitlington and Flockton. The monks of Byland also dealt in iron and were granted rights in Denby and Birstall.

Iron-mining had not in the Middle Ages assumed anything like the importance it was later to have, but relatively speaking it was important. Part, at least, of the early prosperity of Pontefract was due to iron, and possibly the prosperity of Leeds too. Evidence of iron-mining has been found at Horsforth, Middleton and Whitkirk, and there was a flourishing iron industry at Rothwell and Roundhay – there were iron furnaces in Roundhay Park where coal was also obtained. Before the close of the thirteenth century, smelting furnaces had appeared round Wakefield, and in the mid-fourteenth century at Creskeld Park, four miles east of Otley, now the site of a very expensive housing development. There was considerable coal-mining too in the Middle Ages; by 1240 coal was worked near Pontefract, and at Featherstone before the end of Henry III's reign. Outcrops of coal near Birstall were also worked in or about 1287.

During the fourteenth century there was a great increase in the output of West Yorkshire coal, especially round Wakefield and in the Honour of Pontefract. Kippax, Altofts, Allerton, Leeds, Roundhay, Stanley and Walton all became well-established mining centres in the fourteenth century and, as has been proved by excavations, Briggate was bordered by bell pits.

The woollen textile industry, as distinct from the trade in raw wool, was also well established in West Yorkshire during the Middle Ages. Just when, how or by whom the industry was established is not clear. It may have sprung from native sources or it may have been introduced by the Flemings who came in a steady stream during the two centuries following the Conquest. Perusal and analysis of the Poll Tax returns of 1379 show the wool textile industry firmly established in the area.

3

Industry

Long before the Industrial Revolution, the textile area in West Yorkshire had become clearly defined. Its approximate limit in the north was the watershed between the Aire and the Wharfe, while its eastern and southern boundaries were marked by a line joining Leeds, Wakefield and Huddersfield. The region as a whole embraced two different types of area, the Pennine highlands in the west, and further east the more rolling country of the lower valleys of the Aire and Calder. Much of the region, particularly in the west, is highland, lying between five hundred and a thousand feet, and is composed of beds of Millstone Grit separated by impervious shales. The river valleys which dissect the high ground were found by early settlers to be too heavily wooded to allow easy clearance, while the high moorlands were too bleak and inhospitable. The old settlements were therefore in a middle zone; the alternating bands of rock produced a terraced effect so that many of the older settlements, built on the outcrop of hard rock, appear to be perched on a shelf high above the valley.

The moorland terrain was not encouraging for arable or dairy farming but was eminently suitable for sheep-rearing, and the soft water was ideal for washing wool and for dyeing processes, while the swiftly flowing streams provided power to turn wheels for grinding corn or operating the fulling stocks. The common system of farming which lasted in many parts of England until the eighteenth century, and in some until the nineteenth, had never been strong in the Pennine textile region. By the sixteenth century it had almost disappeared.

The textile industry developed and expanded in the sixteenth, seventeenth and eighteenth centuries. Men wishing independently to own small-holdings sought, and frequently obtained, permission to intake and enclose parts of the moorland waste, and individual holdings therefore came into being separate from the townships. Development was not of course uniform; in some places manorial lords held firmly to their rights, and intakes were made much later. These intakes are perpetuated in the word 'royd', another name for 'clearing'. Murgatroyd, for example, means 'moor gate royd'.

That individual enterprise of this nature was able to succeed was due partly to physical reasons and partly to social and economic reasons. The alternating bands of shales and grits ensured a water supply at all levels. The early eighteenth-century traveller Defoe commented that the 'Bounty of Nature' had provided 'running Water upon the Tops of the highest Hills'.[1]

The bleak and inhospitable nature of the area meant that it was unable to support full-time farming, and in order to make a living men needed another occupation. The suitability of sheep to the terrain was no doubt one of the reasons for the beginning of spinning and weaving there, but relatively early in the history of the textile industry the wool produced by the native sheep was insufficient, and wool was imported. There were social reasons too: any system of inheritance in an area of small-scale farming militated against the viability of the small unit. An inheritance based on primogeniture, where the land passed to the eldest son, meant that the younger sons needed to find other means of livelihood. Likewise a system of partable inheritance, where the holding was divided equally between all the sons, ensured that no farm was big enough to provide a livelihood. So in the mid-Pennines textile manufacture was carried on as an adjunct to farming; in the northern Pennines and southern Lake District round Dent, Kirkby Stephen and Kendal, hand knitting was practised, while in the northern Yorkshire Dales, parts of Cumbria and Northumberland lead-mining was carried on. This custom of combining farming with industry was not limited to northerners: it was practised by the nail-makers in Staffordshire and also by textile workers in the West Country, and was common elsewhere in England.

The small freeholders in the Pennines had holdings of between six and fifteen to twenty acres on which they grew oats and potatoes, kept a cow or two for milk, a few hens and a horse. Daniel Defoe noticed this: '. . . so every Manufacturer generally keeps a Cow or two, or more, for his Family, and this employs the two, or three, or four Pieces of enclosed land about his House, for they scarce sow Corn enough for their Cocks and Hens; and this feeding their Grounds still adds by the Dung of the Cattle to enrich the Soil.'[2]

In the villages round Leeds the houses of the clothiers were surrounded by gardens or orchards, and here too were kept swine, a horse or ass, cows and poultry.

The West Yorkshire textile area provided the model of the domestic industry about which an early generation of economic historians wrote such eulogistic prose. Here the industry was not only based physically in the home but its structure and organization were also domestic. The pivots of the industry were the clothier and the fuller, the clothier's family produced the pieces of cloth which he took each week to market. The unit was essentially that of a family, and there was no rank of hired journeyman as in the textile industry in East Anglia and the West Country.

One fleece contained many grades and qualities of wool varying with the breed of sheep and the district, and the first task was to sort the wool. This done, it was washed or scoured in a stream and when dry beaten with rods to loosen any burrs or bits of twig or dead bracken in it. Then it was sprinkled with oil or butter to replace the natural oil lost by washing, and to make easier the carding or combing. The short hairs of the fleece were brushed or carded by the small boys of the family, and the fibres were ultimately made into woollen cloth, but if finer, worsted cloth was to be made, the long fibres were used and were combed. Combing was unhealthy work and was done by men, being carried out with a smoking stove or combers' pot on one side and a cold draught from the open window on the other. The combs weighed five pounds each and contained between three and nine rows of long, sharp teeth. Combers often worked with individual pots – hence the expression 'pot o' one'.

After carding or combing, the wool was ready for the spinner. During spinning the spinster took two or three strides backward to draw out the wool and two or three forward to wind the yarn on the spindle, and during the course of a week's spinning these few strides added up to a total of thirty-three miles walking.

By contrast the weaver had little exercise, his job being cramped and tedious with the need to sit with his body stooping forward over his work. It was a slow process: it took him nearly two hours to weave a yard of coarse cloth. When the piece was taken from the loom, it was washed or scoured to remove the oil and size, this process being carried out at the fulling mill in the valley. The piece was then burled to remove all the knots, and mended, to stitch in the loose ends left by the weaver, after which it was returned to the fulling mill where it was pounded with hammers operated by water power. This process, a mechanical version of trampling or walking the cloth (the origin of the name 'Walker'), caused the cloth to thicken and shrink.

When adequately fulled, the piece was collected by the weaver and dried on tenter frames, which were a feature of every croft. These were long wooden frames with hooks in the upper and lower rails, and the cloth was hooked to the upper rail and then stretched to the lower hooks. Often the cloths were left on the tenters overnight so that they caught the dew, which gave a fine finish to the piece.

The pieces of cloth must have been very tempting to thieves. Anyone in the Halifax area who was caught stealing goods of any description worth 13½d. or more was publicly beheaded on the famous Halifax Gibbet the following Saturday, after having sat in the stocks on any intermediate market days. The well-known Beggars' Litany ran, 'From Hell, Hull and Halifax – deliver us.' (The last trial of the Gibbet was in April 1650. The Gibbet Book says 'that the Gibbet and the Customary Law got its suspension because some Persons in that Age judged it to be too severe'.)

The clothier may have been a small man producing on his own, or with his family, a piece or two each week, carrying it to the market to sell. Or he may have worked in a bigger way, employing more people and doing more of the processes at home. Or he may have been a trading, rather than a manufacturing, clothier, putting out work to spinners and weavers and collecting the finished product.

Cornelius Ashworth, a handloom weaver farming a bit of land with the help of two or three men, possibly relatives, lived at Waltroyd in the Wheatley Valley near Halifax, in the late eighteenth century. His own land had been carved from the waste at an early date, for Waltrode, or 'Walter's clearing', had already been made by 1474. (Further down the valley is Jack-royd, so two quite ordinary people are not forgotten, their names perpetuated in the land they farmed.) Ashworth was in some ways typical of hundreds of men who lived on the hillsides near Halifax, in that he was able to follow his own timetable free from the tyranny of a master. He was an ordinary man, diffident and apparently short of the forcefulness and confidence in his own ability which would have enabled him to make a success of business on a larger scale. But in many respects he was untypi-cal of the eighteenth-century worker: small men of his type were the exception rather than the rule in eighteenth-century Eng-land, which is why they had aroused the interest of Defoe.

One way in which Ashworth was untypical of his fellows was that he kept a diary – from 1782 to 1816, the earliest entry in it is for 4 October 1782, when he would be thirty years old. He combined weaving and farming, some days being spent entirely in farm work while others were divided between the farm and his textile business.

Oct. 24	I churned till 10 o'clock
Thurs.	Wove 6½ yards
Nov. 5th	a fine frosty morning but Overcast and was dull
Tues.	went with my Piece to Halifax and loomed a Warp

He kept livestock, for he spoke of 'fodering' the cows and also churning, and he also grew oats and hay.

Oct. 20	Began fodering the Cows once a day
Sun.	
Oct. 19	a verry high wind with heavy showers of rain
Sat.	and Hail. I and G. Town Winowed 13 quarters of oats
Oct. 18	3 men and myself and Thomas Marsden Housed
Fri.	78 Hattocks of Corn between 7 o'clock and a little past 9 o' clock in the forenoon. I and George Town mooed before noon and thrasht in the Afternoon[3]

The hattock to which he referred was a shock of standing sheaves of corn. The tops of the sheaves were protected by two sheaves laid along them, their ends touching in the centre and their heads slanting downwards in order to carry off the rain. The sheltering sheaves were originally the hattock, the cap or hat.

His diary is punctuated with the homely touches about little jobs which formed the daily round, the common task. Some were on his own account:

> Oct. 23   Clouted my Coat in the Evening [i.e. patched]
> Wed.
> July 2nd   weeded garden and other jobbs
> Wed.
> July 11th . . . Carried my Piece
> Fri.   mended Rake

And he gave a helping hand to others:

> July 5th   . . . helped Jas Charnock to
> Sat.   flit in afternoon[4]

Although we know he carried his piece to Halifax, he did not say where. He seems to have gone on different days – Monday, Tuesday, Wednesday and Friday, and as market day at the Piece Hall was Saturday, it is likely that the work he did was that which was put out to him. Tradition has it that on Monday and Tuesday the handloom went to the chant of 'Plenty of time, plenty of time', but on Thursday and Friday work had to be speeded up and the loom clacked, 'A day t'lat, a day t' lat'.

Ashworth was a deeply religious man, attending each week at Square Chapel, an independent Methodist chapel where Titus Knight was the minister. Between services men and women who came from Wheatley repaired to the 'Boar's Head', where they fortified themselves with penny bowls of soup and the havercake which they had brought with them. Although not sparked off by spirituous liquor, they would doubtless have a lively time exchanging the news and gossip of the week. Once a month the minister came to Waltroyd, where Ashworth played host not only to the minister but also to his own neighbours who came to the farmhouse service. The Baptist minister also attended in Wheatley although not necessarily at Waltroyd, and it is likely that Ashworth attended his services too, as he changed his denomination from Methodist to Baptist, being baptized on 17 April 1795.

A clothier who worked in a much bigger way than Cornelius Ashworth was Sam Hill, who lived at Soyland. The fragments of his letter books which remain are available only for a period of three weeks in 1737. During this time he sold almost a thousand pieces of cloth, which must have necessitated his employing at least two hundred weavers.

From the fourteenth century the most important cloth in the Halifax area had been the kersey, a cheap, coarse woollen cloth made in white, blue, red and other colours. It was a serviceable cloth, able to keep out wet and cold, and was in demand in many parts of Europe as it was the material for the clothing of the poorer classes. In the early centuries a piece had been about sixteen to eighteen yards in length and less than a yard wide, but by the eighteenth century many kerseys were woven over forty yards long. Similar in quality was the Pennistone, which was always worn in white and was ¾ yards wide. Sam Hill dealt in kerseys, selling various qualities and marketing them under the names of members of his family.

. . . I sell my Kers[ys] as under	
Sx Hx	at 30
James Hill	at 33½
Sam Hill	at 37
Richard Hill	at 39
Elizabeth Hill	at 41
Sam and Eliz. Hill	at 50
Sam Hill of Soyland	at 56
Samuel Hill of Soyland	at 60[5]

Newer fabrics were the bay, a light, coarse fabric, half woollen and half worsted, and the shalloon, a light worsted fabric used for lining coats and for women's dresses. The manufacture of bays was firmly established in West Yorkshire by the beginning of the eighteenth century, and manufacturers were beginning to

make shalloons. Breaking into a new market was a daunting
task, and Sam Hill on his hillside must have often felt dispirited:
'. . . am perfectly sick of the little or no hope of the Shalloon
business.'[6] There were times when he must have felt almost
intolerably lonely and cut off from the mainstream of business:
'It wod be a great pleasure if you wod please soon to take the
freedom of staying one Night with me here. I want an Hours
chat by ourselves most Sadly.'[7]

Sam Hill was the son of James and Deborah Hill of Soyland;
he was born in or about 1677 and was about twenty-nine years
old when he obtained Making Place. It was not on the site of the
present building but some little distance away, and Sam Hill
was a relatively poor man at the time he acquired it. He had a
strong personality, a capacity for hard work and perseverance,
and he amassed great wealth through his cloth business. The
Making Place he built was of a size and architectural style quite
alien to buildings in the moorland townships, although func-
tionally it was similar to many other dwelling-places of large
clothiers. The older buildings were converted into workshops;
warehouses and farm buildings were built and tentercrofts
made. Eventually he acquired other property in the area.

His trade was large and was varied in both range and extent.
His pattern book shows the range of his manufactures – there
were everlastings, coloured kerseys, grograins, calamancoes
and amens, to mention but some. And his markets were both
local and foreign: his goods went to Amsterdam, Rotterdam,
Utrecht, Antwerp and Bremen, and he also supplied cloth to St
Petersburg. His annual turnover was between £25,000 and
£30,000. Of his children only Richard survived him, and it was
Richard who was at one time responsible for the advent into the
business of John Collier – alias Tim Bobbin, the Lancashire
poet, who was employed as head clerk at Kebroyd. The appoint-
ment lasted for only three years as Tim Bobbin found the work
too humdrum. It may not have lasted longer than that anyway,
as Sam Hill was furious at the magnitude of the salary Richard
had paid Bobbin.

He also disliked Richard's wife and was determined that his
money should not go to her children. Litigation about his will
continued after his death until 1793, a period of thirty-four

years. Richard died, practically penniless, in Bremen in 1780.

It was during the eighteenth century also that technological change was felt in the textile industry. On an average it needed five or six spinners to keep a weaver supplied with yarn, and often he must have been prevented from getting a piece off the loom because of the famine in yarn. When narrow cloth, one yard wide, was woven, a weaver worked single-handed, throwing the shuttle through the shed (the gap in the strands of warp), catching it at the other side and returning it. The production of broad cloth, 1¾ yards wide, required two men working together – one to return the shuttle.

Three of the key inventions which helped to bring about a revolution in industry were made by Lancastrians. The patenting, in 1733, by John Kay, who was born near Bury, of his flying shuttle, a device whereby the weaver, pulling a cord, could return the shuttle automatically, meant that work which had previously needed two men could now be done by one. It also intensified the famine in yarn. About 1764 James Hargreaves, who was probably a native of Blackburn, invented a jenny enabling a spinner to work eight spindles simultaneously. This was patented in 1770, when the patent specification mentioned sixteen spindles; by 1784 the number had increased to eighty, and by the end of the century modifications and adaptations to the machine made it capable of holding between 100 and 120 spindles.

These inventions were almost immediately popular and were widely adopted, especially in the cotton textile industry, but they were not instigators of an industrial revolution. Dependent in no way on power other than that of the human hand, they were suitable for use in the home. It was the invention of the water frame by Richard Arkwright, a barber from Preston, which was the true pioneer of a revolution in the textile industry. The water frame used for spinning was patented in 1769.

Worked at first by animal power and later by water, Arkwright's spinning frame began the departure from cottage industry. More important to the woollen industry was another invention of Arkwright: a carding machine, perfected by him in 1775.

As a result of the adoption of Arkwright's machines, spinning

mills and scribbling mills were established, existing corn or
fulling mills being adapted to this use, while new buildings were
also erected. In August 1785 we read in the diary of Cornelius
Ashworth that Charles Crowther undertook the cleaning and
enlarging of the mill dam at Jumples Mill and that Mr
Ashworth helped with the work. On 14 January 1786 it was
reared, and the rearing feast was at Savile Green that night.

The name 'Jumples' has a Yorkshire flavour to it – and there
is still a mill there, although not the same mill. There are
several Jumple holes in the Halifax parish, and the place is
always associated with a narrow, wooded clough where the beck
tumbles over rocks. It may be that the word derived from the
jumble of boulders, water and vegetation, or it may refer to the
stream jumping down in small cascades. This terrain is typical
of many small valleys in the area and was of course ideal for the
early mills. Mr Ashworth and several others investigated the
possibilities of opening a mill at Triangle but they did not get
the contract. Jumples Mill and other mills erected in his lifetime would, of course, have been spinning mills. The narrow,
steepsided valleys with their small, swiftly flowing streams
were ideal for small mills which harnessed the power of the
water to work the machines.

Industry and population drifted into the valleys, and new
towns grew up round the fulling mills and their bridges – for
example Sowerby Bridge, Brighouse, Hebden Bridge and Milns-
bridge. Eventually steam power replaced water power, and
more and bigger mills came into being.

Much of the labour for the factories was provided by children,
and a great deal of prose has been written and emotion generated about the cruelty which was alleged to have prevailed
there. There *was* cruelty in some factories, and children were
beaten and strapped, but generally speaking in West Yorkshire
mills more widespread harm was caused by working conditions
than by actual cruelty. Ordinary hours of work were 12½ to
thirteen a day, while it was common to find children of nine, ten
and eleven who worked from fourteen to fifteen hours. Much
more common than injury caused by cruel treatment was the
stunted growth and deformity to limbs caused by long hours of
standing. Deformity of the knee was especially common in the

worsted spinning mills and was produced by the posture it was necessary to adopt in stopping the spindle for piecing. The most prevalent cause of deformity was the excessively long hours of work.

The increasing use of steam power meant that more coal was needed. Coal-mining was another staple industry of West Yorkshire. The monastic houses had been the first entrepreneurs, and after the dissolution of the monasteries their mining enterprises were continued. Minerals were the property of the person who owned the land, and for a long time it was the practice for owners to lease mines for a share of the coal, although by the eighteenth century money rents were common. Sometimes these were in addition to coal, and often there was also an understanding that the site would be cleaned up when mining operations had finished.

By the end of the eighteenth century Yorkshire and Lancashire industry was estimated to use about 1½ million tons of coal annually. Colliers were amongst the highest-paid workers at that time. In 1786 their wages were 2s. 6d. to 3s. a day for an eight-hour day; not one of them earned less than 2s. a day.

As the Industrial Revolution gathered momentum and more steam engines were employed in the factories, the demand for coal increased and the mines, like the factories, used child labour. The employment of very young children underground was common; an instance of a child of three, another between four and five and another between five and six was recorded in the Halifax area. There were several who started work at the age of seven.

In the Bradford, Halifax and Mirfield area many mines except those belonging to the great companies were poorly ventilated, and some were so badly drained that people, children included, worked in mud and water. The chief employment of children underground was as trappers. They sat in a little hole scooped out for them in the side of the gates behind each door. In their hands they held a piece of string which was attached to the door, and as soon as they heard the corves (carriages) of coal, they pulled the string to open the door. The moment the corve had passed, they let the door fall to. They sat in the dark on a damp floor, and the hours of work were between ten and eleven per day with often no regular mealtime. The children took what food they could and 'ate on the job'.

Existing slagheaps and pithead gear provide evidence of mining activity, and mills remain to indicate the presence of the textile industry. It is in the western valleys that the pattern of the historical development of the textile industry is still evident. Weavers' cottages like those at Waltroyd near Halifax are found on the hillsides or are present in upland villages such as Sowerby in Calderdale, and Holme and Upperthong in the Holme valley. They are sturdy and attractive, many dating back to the seventeenth century. Most retain the long rows of mullioned windows, some having more than a dozen lights, although, in the name of progress and for ease of window-cleaning and economy of electricity, some householders have removed the mullions and put in larger panes.

There are rows of cottages with no outbuildings – the houses of the weavers who worked as employees of the big clothiers; typical are those in Heptonstall. Other buildings appear to be clustered, and in addition to the dwelling-house there are farm buildings and outhouses. One would have been used for the farm animals and gear, one for combing, another as a dyehouse. There is an example of such a farm near Mytholmroyd in Calderdale; it can be seen quite easily from the main road. An addition of the eighteenth century would be a warehouse or 'Takkin in shop' where the spun yarn would be brought and stored until needed, for after the invention of the jenny there was a superfluity of yarn. And there are the bigger houses of the large clothiers such as Kershaw House in the Luddenden Valley, a quarter of a mile from the main road between Halifax and Todmorden; Holdsworth House at Holmfield, Halifax, and Ovenden Hall at Ovenden, near Halifax. Many of these clothiers' homes are superb examples of seventeenth-century vernacular architecture.

Many of the mills which were built in the valleys were fine buildings and stand well: there are good examples at Marsden and Slaithwaite, at Elland, Greetland and West Vale. Some mills, built in the later nineteenth century were real architectural gems, notably Manningham Mills and Salt's Mill at Saltaire. The works at Saltaire cover an area of 9¾ acres, the principal buildings being in the form of a letter T, the horizontal stroke representing the mill while the perpendicular stroke was the warehouse. Built of stone in an Italian style, the mill is so impressive that a visitor commented that it had a palatial appearance and wondered what the Plantagenets would say if they could come back and find trade using palaces far more stately than those of kings.[8] Because of the recent recession in the textile industry, much of the space in the mill is unused. The latest idea is to convert much of the space into flats, using capital provided by private investors, local authorities and central government.

Titus Salt's palace of industry was opened in September 1853. A grand inaugural banquet was held in the combing shed, a room which provided seating accommodation for 3,500 guests, among whom were 2,440 of his workpeople who had been brought from Bradford by special train, several noblemen and members of Parliament.

In 1871 Manningham Mills were destroyed by fire and were replaced with a new building, an immense structure covering 16 acres of flooring with a frontage of 350 yards and extending backwards for a distance of 150 yards. But it is the chimney which is the most impressive feature, a square structure 83 yards in height and with 7,000 tons of material used in its construction. Like Titus Salt, Lister seems to have been impressed by Italian architecture, and it was probably the belfry tower of St Mark in Venice which suggested that the great shaft of the chimney. The huge double cornice almost at the top of the shaft gives an impression of solidity which is more imposing than the tapering belfry of St Mark's.

Both Saltaire Mill and Manningham Mill are immensely impressive. Seen from the main road, it is the church, rather than the mill in Saltaire, which dominates the village. Low-lying, the mill is on the banks of the canal, in the valley bottom, and one needs to see it from a height to appreciate its size and the atmosphere of power which it conveys. Seen across the valley from the opposite hillside, it is at its most impressive. Manningham Mill, on the other hand, is on a hill and is clearly visible from many parts of the area, where it appears to dominate the city.

The enterprise of Cornelius Ashworth and Sam Hill was followed by later generations of textile entrepreneurs, a notable example being the Fielden family of Todmorden. The Fieldens were an old-established local family able to trace an unbroken descent from a Nicholas Fielden who was a yeoman holding a farm at Inchfield in Walsden in the early seventeenth century. Joshua Fielden was a yeoman farmer who, having two or three handlooms, combined cloth-manufacture with farming at Edge End. He carried his pieces on his back to market in Halifax, walking, there and back, a distance of twenty-four miles. No doubt he would call on his way at one or two houses for rest and probably refreshment, and one of the farms at which he called was Rodwell End, where the Greenwood family lived. Eventually Joshua married one of the daughters of the family, Jenny.

In 1782 he abandoned his trade of woollen cloth manufacture and decided to become a cotton-spinner. He moved from Edge End to Lane Side in the valley, where the family occupied three two-storeyed cottages, living in one of them and making the other two into the working place. At first they confined themselves to the hand spinning of cotton and managed to keep consistently employed, which was quite an achievement. Children arrived and eventually they had a family of five sons and four daughters, the boys, Samuel, Joshua, John, James and Thomas, joining the business as soon as they were old enough. In business the family had a unity of purpose: they all pulled one way, which quality, combined with honesty and hard work, accounted for the success of their firm.

Gradually and cautiously they expanded their premises as business increased. First they added a storey to the three cottages, and later, when they decided to use steam power, they built a stone mill of five storeys and seven windows in length adjoining the cottages. Each of the sons was allotted a special department in the business, the father superintending the whole. Joshua was the mechanic, James was in charge of spinning and weaving, Thomas went to Manchester to take charge of a warehouse there and John saw to the buying of cotton and selling the manufactured goods. Each Tuesday he went with his father to Manchester market, a distance of forty miles there and back. They left home at four o'clock in the morning and arrived back in Todmorden at midnight the same day, after having walked both ways.

In 1811 Joshua died and the name of the firm was changed to Fielden Brothers, while at some time after the death of Samuel in 1822 the premises became known as Waterside. Year by year the premises expanded: at first the waterwheel had been the motive power, then a steam-engine, at first a small one and then by degrees bigger and bigger engines. In 1829 a large weaving shed was erected capable of housing eight hundred looms; at the time of its erection it was the largest shed in the world. More spinning mills were built and a second and larger weaving shed was put up. About 1844 warehouses were built along the side of the Lancashire and Yorkshire Railway, and a railway siding was brought right into the works. In addition to the main works at Waterside, individual members of the family bought from time to time smaller mills – all used for spinning – in the valleys which ran up into the hills from the main valley.

When Joshua Fielden began cotton-spinning, the amount used was small, the weekly consumption not averaging more than could be brought from Manchester in a horse and cart. As the means of transport improved and the business expanded, the amount of raw cotton also increased. In 1846 some four hundred bales, each containing five hundred pounds, were used each week. In 1830 gasworks were erected to light the factory premises, this being the first gasworks to be established by any private firm.

The Fieldens were model employers. At the time of the Civil War in the USA in the early 1860s, the price of raw cotton was very high, and the practice became prevalent in the cotton industry of sizing the cotton. This the Fieldens refused to do as they believed in selling honest cotton cloth rather than material which had been dressed to make it appear to be something it was not. Eventually, however, they had to adopt the policy of selling sized cotton as they were being undercut by other manufacturers and would eventually have had to go out of business. The Fieldens were so transparently honest that, had it not been for their sense of obligation to their employees, two thousand of them, who would have been out of jobs, they would really rather have ceased business than use dubious work practices.

As it was, in the period of the cotton famine, they found it necessary to close their works for nine months, during which time they allowed the workers to come to the mill once a week to clean the machinery and paid them half their ordinary wages. They set large numbers of them to work in reclaiming waste land for the sake of giving them an occupation, and sewing schools were established for the women.

As early as 1816 John had championed the cause of the factory workers and striven to obtain better conditions for them. Hours at the Fielden brothers' works were shorter than those worked elsewhere, and the brothers would have liked them to be shorter still, but they found they could not compete with other factories if they reduced the hours to be out of line with their competitors. In 1832 John became MP for Oldham, and in 1847 he put through the second reading of the Ten Hour Bill.

In 1847 Joshua Fielden died, followed by John in 1849 and James in 1852, leaving the one remaining brother, Thomas, to carry on the business. This he did with John's three sons, Sam, John and Joshua, until his death in 1869. The family firm flourished for many years, and the brothers continued the spirit of benevolence by using their money to enrich their native town.

Other textile barons were instrumental in pushing forward the frontiers of knowledge about new machines and new yarns. One was Samuel Cunliffe Lister, son of the MP for Bradford in 1832, Ellis Cunliffe Lister, who had moved to Manningham Hall about fifteen years earlier. Samuel Cunliffe Lister, who had been born in 1815 at Calverley Hall near Leeds, was then a child of two or three, and it was intended that he would take Holy Orders. Samuel, however, had different ideas. He was fascinated by the rapidly expanding world of industry and commerce, and when he left school, he spurned his father's suggestion of university and instead acquired a position in the counting house at Messrs Sands, Turner & Co of Liverpool. While working there he made several voyages to the USA. When he came of age, he prevailed on his brother to enter into business with him at Manningham. Their father built them a mill but after two years John, Samuel's brother, retired from the partnership, and Samuel instead took James Ambler in.

At this time wool-combing was done by hand, for the production of a satisfactory machine defied the ingenuity of inventors. Lister took into partnership a Mr Donnisthorpe who had invented a machine for combing wool, and by working together they eventually produced a machine which was acceptable to the trade. Lister became a sort of wool-comber king, having command of one entire branch of worsted manufacture. The works at Manningham were enlarged and branch establishments set up elsewhere in the area, notably at Halifax and Keighley, and Lister even established works in France. And all the time he was restlessly at work trying to improve the wool-combing machine.

It was while he was in London that he stumbled on the embryo of his second great invention. In a warehouse there he happened to notice a pile of rubbish and on asking about it he was told that it was silk waste which was just sold off cheaply. He poked about in it and must have had some idea of being able to use it as he eventually offered a halfpenny a pound for it. On reaching Bradford he spent some time analysing and investigating his purchase, and on finding that silk waste all the world over was just treated as rubbish, he set himself to find a profitable use for it. His aim was to invent machinery which would re-cycle the waste and transform it into fabrics. Unlike his previous work on the wool-combing machine, his idea for silk was not beset by rivals.

Lister engaged workmen from abroad who at first viewed him and his apparently mad idea with deep suspicion but eventually came to share with him the belief that the idea was not totally impossible. He spent £360,000 in perfecting machinery to process silk waste before ever making a penny profit. By 1865 he had accomplished the task and was able to make beautiful velvet. Velvet-manufacture needed a special loom, and this too had to be perfected, so Lister found that he had to invent not one machine but many in order to realize his dream of converting silk waste into material.

Lister used his wealth to help the people of Bradford. As the town had no park, he threw open the grounds of Manningham Hall to the public every Whitsuntide for the celebration of the holiday. He made a small admission charge in order to raise a fund for some of the charitable institutions in the city. In 1870 he sold the mansion and the park to the corporation for £40,000.

It was on the advice of Isaac Holden that Lister eventually introduced his wool-combing machine to his works in France. Holden was slightly older than Lister and unlike him was not a Yorkshireman, being born in Scotland; also unlike Lister, he had no advantages of wealth behind him but came from a very humble background. His father had had a small farm at Nent-head near Alston, being a farmer and lead-miner, but the eventual exhaustion of the lead mines meant that he needed to find alternative employment and so, in 1801, he moved to Glasgow. Here he got employment as a collier, eventually becoming headsman, and it was here that Isaac was born. The child had a rather chequered early life as his father seemed constantly to need to move in order to find work.

Isaac was sent to school, and his father was keen for him to have a good education; but a well-developed conscience urged him to leave school and seek work whenever the family fortunes were at a low ebb. When he was fifteen, after various periods in and out of school and work alike, he was apprenticed to a shawl-weaver. As he approached manhood, two things happened which meant that his young adulthood was to be almost as varied as his childhood: the shawl-making proved to be too much for his health so that he gave it up to become a full-time student and eventually a teacher, and he became deeply religious. His deep and firm religious convictions did not endear him to his colleagues, and his years in teaching saw moves from school to school as his religious views failed to harmonize with those of his employers. In 1830 he took a post in Glasgow as a schoolmaster, and it was while he was there that he met William Townend, a member of a firm at Cullingworth near Bingley who was looking for someone to engage as a book-keeper. A friend recommended Isaac Holden and so, in November 1830, he went to Cullingworth. It was while he was in Cullingworth that he was taken by Townend to see a hand wool-comber and became fired with the idea of producing a wool-combing machine. So engrossed did he become with this idea that in 1846 he left Cullingworth and moved to Bradford.

It was inevitable that he and Lister should meet, and Holden was sure that he could improve Lister's wool-combing machine so as to make it useful for merino wools. The outcome of all this was that Lister and Holden agreed to begin combing in partnership in France. There never was a more sudden and complete transformation brought about in any branch of industry than this that was wrought in wool-combing. Thousands of combers were left without employment – Messrs Townend had themselves kept seven hundred handcombers going – and it was the same in France. When Lister and Holden began their work in St Denis, wool-combing was done chiefly by peasant farmers in their own homes.

The business of Lister and Holden flourished and further improvements in the machines were made, Holden in 1850 bringing out his 'square motion' machine. Abroad they expanded their enterprises, establishing works at Rheims and Croix. Of course there were others interested in the wool-combing machines and their adaptations, and attempts were made to pirate those invented by Holden, so much so that he was involved in numerous lawsuits about patents and often had to come across the Channel to England. Lister, in 1858, retired from his French concerns and proposed to sell his share to Holden, who in 1859 relinquished his interest in the works and set up the Alston works in Bradford.

Titus Salt's career had more than one parallel with that of Lister. He was born at Morley in 1803 and shortly afterwards his father, a farmer, moved to Crofton near Wakefield, later going to Bradford where he became a wool-stapler. Young Titus's ideas about a career differed from those of his father, and in this he was like Samuel Lister, but unlike Lister he eventually did what his father wanted. Titus hankered after a farmer's life but his father thought otherwise and he became a partner in the family firm in 1834. However, he threw himself into the business wholeheartedly and was soon making experiments and encouraging others to do the same. He became interested in Donskoi, a Russian fleece which had been used in the manufacture of wool. Although it had hitherto been regarded as unsuitable for worsted-manufacture, Salt was sure it could be used for this and urged the Bradford spinners to try. They were unwilling to experiment, and so Salt set up as a worsted spinner at an old mill, determined to put his theory into practice. Eventually he succeeded in producing good worsted cloth. Meanwhile others were experimenting with alpaca wool.

In 1836, on one of his wool-buying expeditions, Salt came across a sack of alpaca waste and asked the head of the firm if he would accept 8d. a pound for it. Having got it, he adapted and altered and invented and processed until eventually he produced material which became as amenable to the machine as sheep's wool. Orders poured in and soon Salt was carrying on the manufacture of alpaca at four separate mills in four separate parts of Bradford. Between 1836 and 1840 the quantity of alpaca wool imported averaged 560,800 pounds per annum; by 1852 the amount had risen to 2,186,480 pounds, and by 1872 to 3,878,739 pounds. The price commanded by alpaca wool had also risen; in 1836 Salt had paid 8d. a pound, and by 1856 the price was 2s. 6d.

In 1844 he received two fleeces from alpacas which were kept on the royal farm at Windsor. They weighed 16½ pounds and when sorted and combed yielded one pound of white and nine pounds of black wool. From this material he manufactured an apron; a striped figured dress, the warp of rose-coloured silk and the weft of white alpaca; a plain dress fifteen yards in length; a plaid alpaca dress and a woollen alpaca dress. Queen Victoria was delighted, and from that time alpaca constituted an article of royal costume.

However, the late 1880s the fashion trade was beginning to move away from mohair and alpaca, and colonial wools were therefore introduced for the production of high-class worsted coatings and soft dress cloths, a trade which has continued until the present day.

Bradford was no less delighted with its famous citizen and when, in 1847, the city was incorporated, Salt was made senior alderman and one of the first JPs, while in 1848 he was chosen Mayor.

During his lifetime, Salt was the sole owner of the company but after his death in 1876 all surviving members of his family became shareholders. In 1881 the firm was registered as a limited liability company under the name Sir Titus Salt, Baronet, Sons Company Limited.

By the early 1890s there were financial difficulties, and in 1892 it was agreed that the existing company should be wound up and receivers called in, a tragedy which appalled many local people. However, a syndicate of four Bradford businessmen was formed to purchase the company and its assets, assuming control in June 1893. Individual members of the Salt family continued to own shares. The mill was modernized and extended; new engines and machinery were bought, and by 1895 trade was once again buoyant.

The firm, under varying managements, prospered until it, like many others, was hit by the slump of 1929–30. Overheads were pruned; capital was written down; Saltaire village was sold to a Bradford estate agent, and the company was thus relieved of the burden of maintaining domestic property. The firm cut its losses and began to prosper so that in 1933 activity was greater than for some time past. Other mills were bought and activities diversified. This prosperity continued during the Second World War and beyond.

In 1958 ordinary shares of the Salts (Saltaire) Ltd group of companies were acquired by Illingworth Morris & Co Ltd, who still produce textiles there.

Generally West Yorkshire's woollen and worsted industry suffered much less in the 1930s than the cotton industry. There has, however, been considerable contraction in the 1970s and 1980s. Many mills have been adapted for light industry, and West Yorkshire is relying on an increasing tourist industry partly at least to take the place of textiles.

4

Transport

The railway era ushered in an age of mobility: industrial raw materials were transported more speedily and so were finished products; standard brick and slate began to replace local stone for building; mails were speeded up and London newspapers became available in the provinces. It was increasingly easy for people to move; whereas previously men and women had been born, lived and worked and died in the same village, it was now possible for them to move further afield in search of work. It was also easier for people to go on holiday and on day excursions – many seaside towns developed because of the railways.

This does not mean, however, that there was no movement of people before the advent of railways. Certainly there was not the mass movement of people; but then there were not the masses of people.

Monastic activities must have accounted for considerable traffic. It is true that, apart from Kirkstall Abbey, the great Cistercian houses were situated outside West Yorkshire, but their considerable agricultural and manufacturing activities in the county generated traffic in goods and people, and there were also many smaller monastic establishments.

Medieval kings and their courts were frequent travellers to and from their manors, and so too were the tenants-in-chief of the realm, both lay and spiritual. Pontefract, as the head-quarters of the de Laci fee, and Sandal Castle, guarding the northern interests of the Warenes, must have had considerable traffic. Although cases were regularly tried elsewhere, the most important courts were held at Pontefract and Wakefield, and to them came those who owed 'suit of court' to the lord (compulsory attendance at his court). (In the Manor of Wakefield the freehold

Adel Church, Leeds, in winter sunshine

The west front of Kirkstall Abbey with its splendid Norman doorway

Waltroyd, near Halifax, at one time the home of Cornelius Ashworth

Mills overlooking the Colne valley at Marsden

A superb stretch
of causey from
Mankinholes over the
shoulder of Stoodley
Pike and down into
Cragg Vale

Market at the Piece
Hall, Halifax

Colonnade, the Piece
Hall, Halifax

Todmorden Town Hall

The Library, Pontefract

Crowds at Pontefract market, one of the most delightful of West Yorkshire's markets

Todmorden, from the hillside below Stoodley Pike

Hebden Bridge, like a Tibetan monastery—a town where the houses seem to cling to the hillside

The Colne Valley from Pule Hill, Marsden

Walsden village—a community which grew out of the Industrial Revolution

Victoria Road, Saltaire,
one of the most well-known
streets in Titus Salt's villag

The church at Saltaire
which seems to
dominate the village

tenants had to do suit at the manor court, and they were fined for default unless they had excused themselves by giving some reason for their absence which could be accepted by the steward. A freeholder could appoint an attorney to do suit for him, and the attorney was subject to the same necessity of doing suit or making his excuse [essoign]. Many freeholders paid a lump sum to be excused doing suit for a fixed period.) And there were widespread markets and fairs throughout the county; the merchants who attended the great fairs of the realm must have been constantly on the road, as must, more locally, the pedlars and hawkers who travelled to isolated farms. The drovers who attended fairs were another section of the community who were frequently on the roads.

With the expansion of the woollen industry in the seventeenth century, packhorse traffic developed, but the trains of packhorses were not a distinctive feature either of West Yorkshire or of the seventeenth century. Trains of packhorses were certainly travelling in other parts of the country before 1500 but it was not until the seventeenth century that the long trains of packhorses became a fairly common sight. Packhorse traffic survived longer in the north than in the south of England.

Many of the old packhorse roads have been incorporated into modern metalled and widened roads, and it is often difficult to trace their exact route. In the Calderdale region, where it is possible to trace a considerable number of packhorse tracks still on the ground, it was usual to refer to them as lanes, and this description was incorporated into the subsequent turnpike roads. So any section of a turnpike road – now a main road – called 'lane' was probably at one time part of a packhorse road. 'Bank' is another word surviving from packhorse days, which indicates a one-time packhorse track, 'bank' meaning a lane climbing a hill, as well as the hill itself. 'Gate' indicates a road which was traversed by pedlars – Easter Gate from Marsden over into Lancashire was a road which was usually open at Easter after the heavy snow.

Characteristic of the packhorse tracks were the causeys – narrow pavements raised from the ground. They were efficient highways and must have been fairly easy to follow in misty weather, their only drawback being their narrowness. It was of

course possible, if two packhorse trains met, for one of them to
step aside into the mud alongside the causey, but there must
have been interesting altercations before one train gave way.
Kildwick Bridge was approached by a causey 644 feet long and
was 'built with rough stones and paved with boulders'. There is a
superb stretch of causey from Mankinholes over the shoulder of
Stoodley Pike and down into Cragg Vale, and another across the
moor under the shadow of Whirlaw rocks. These one-time
packhorse routes make splendid tracks on which to walk, some
taking one through deep woodland, for example that to Lumb
Bridge and that through Callis Woods. Their substance makes
one realize the vast volume of traffic they at one time carried.
Others snake enticingly across the moors and hillsides – from
Mankinholes at the foot of Stoodley Pike to Hebden Bridge, for
instance, and also that from Blackshaw Head going into the
Kebs Road, and the one from Ramsden Clough over to Wardle,
and another from Pecket Well into Crimsworth Dean. One of the
mysteries is who paid for the upkeep of these tracks. The
packhorses that tramped them were usually Galloways; their
normal load was 240 pounds carried in two panniers of 120
pounds each.

A pressing need was for the provision of bridges where the
tracks crossed streams, and the practice grew of wealthy
clothiers leaving money in their wills for such bridges to be
provided. Some of them are very fine structures, for example,
Lumb Bridge in Crimsworth Dean and Beckfoot Bridge, Bingley. Now metalled is the track across the Aire at Beckfoot,
Bingley, which leads into the (now) main road to Harden. This
was the route of the monks from Rievaulx Abbey who had
interest in an iron works at Harden.

There were certain definite routes used by drovers as they
travelled from fair to fair, and like the packhorse tracks these
kept to the high ground to avoid the heavily wooded valleys.
Like packhorse tracks too, many of them have subsequently
been metalled and are now difficult to trace. Part of one drovers'
route followed an old road from York to Kendal. Drovers coming
from Malham and Bordley fairs and travelling south would
make first for Skipton; then, to avoid paying toll on the valley
road, they would take the route over the hills from Skipton,

eventually reaching Cringles Top. From Cringles Top they went to Windgate Nick and across to Doubler Stones and Black Pots farm, which was once a licensed house known as 'Gaping Goose'. From here they would proceed across the moorland, which provided good pasture for their animals, ford the stream and join the Morton to Silsden road near Holden Gate. They would then go to Bingley via East Morton, and from Bingley to Wibsey.

Packhorse traffic reached its peak about 1750 and from then dwindled; by the end of the eighteenth century it had been ousted by the wagon, the stage-coach and the canal barge. Packhorses had been adequate for the industrial system of the sixteenth and seventeenth centuries but, just as the technological changes of the second half of the eighteenth century needed a new system of industrial organization, so they called into being a new system of transport. Packhorses were no longer adequate to carry the amount of goods. In the Pennine region, as the population began to desert the hilltop settlements for the valleys, the new transport system ran along the valleys rather than across the hills.

Packhorse tracks were officially referred to as the Common Highway or the King's Highway, the latter term evoking a vision of a superb network of roads connecting north to south and east to west all the main administrative centres, a sort of medieval motorway system. But this is to construe the phrase wrongly, for the term King's Highway in fact meant a road which had the right of passage for the king and his subjects over the land of someone else. The physical condition of the road in any case would have left much to be desired. For, to the medieval mind, a road was like a person suffering from a minor indisposition – left alone, it would right itself of its own accord.

With the decay of the feudal system, administration of local affairs passed from the lord of the manor to the township; it became the custom for the people of the township to keep order within its bounds, to look after the poor in their midst, to administer justice and to repair the highways. Custom was regularized by various Acts of Parliament; that relating to roads was given statutory authority by the Highways Act of 1555 – all male parishioners were to give six days' labour per year on the

roads. The work was organized and co-ordinated by the Over-
seer of the Highways, who was himself a householder of the
parish; it was unpaid and, if properly done, onerous, but the
holder of the office, who was appointed annually by the vestry
meeting round about each Easter, had no qualifications for
his task. He may have been a victualler, grocer or blacksmith,
and he was not always literate, needing help in measuring or
even in writing up his accounts. In such places where the work
was tackled enthusiastically, it would not necessarily have
knowledge or expertise behind it. No wonder the roads were
– in most parts of England – in an execrable condition, evoking
passages of purple prose from those who wrote about their
travels.

Turnpike trusts were set up in an attempt to improve conditions on the roads. The first instance of one appeared in 1706,
and its function was to keep in repair existing roads rather than
make new ones. In most cases a private Act of Parliament
permitted a body of trustees to maintain and manage an existing highway. The trustees usually included the landowners
and people of standing who lived along the particular section of
road. They were empowered to set up toll gates and levy certain
specified tolls on all road-users. From these tolls they were able
to keep the road in a state of good repair.

In the first instance turnpike trusts did not make new roads.
They charged tolls to people to travel on roads where previously
they had travelled without paying any toll, and therefore it is
easy to understand why they were not popular. To get stuck in a
deep rut and then be expected to pay for the experience seemed
to be adding insult to injury. They were also permitted to use
statute labour for the repair of the roads. When turnpike trusts
decided to make a diversion – that was their way of referring to a
new stretch of road – they raised the necessary money in loan
capital. They advertised in the papers for loans, offering 4½ or 5
per cent interest, the security being the income from tolls; the
trustees themselves were not personally liable.

In the turnpike era it was not easy for would-be investors to
find safe and profitable securities for their capital, and therefore
turnpike trusts were regarded with favour. It was unfortunate
for many of these investors that the unexpected, in the shape of

railways, came onto the scene, drawing traffic away from the roads so that in the long run the investors suffered, finding themselves cast in the role of public benefactors.

In the early days the trustees relied on their own nominees, probably their servants, to collect the tolls, paying them a small sum and expecting them to be on duty for long hours – 4 a.m. to 11 p.m. was usual. The toll-keeper at Baitings got 7s. 6d. a week, at Sowerby Bridge the same, while the man at King Cross got only 3s. The system was abandoned after a short trial, and the plan of letting the tolls was adopted. The right of collecting the tolls was put up for sale by auction and sold to the highest bidder, who thus became the farmer of the tolls at one or more of the gates. After paying the collectors, he had for himself the balance between the sum received from the total tolls collected and the sum he had paid the trustees. Toll letting was not a dry procedure: quantities, probably considerable, of spiritous liquor were consumed and the occasion no doubt was very lively.

Physical remains of the turnpike era exist throughout the county. There are many examples of 'bar' used in directions in road reports on the radio, and as bus-stops: Chain Bar, Bar Lane, Cottingley Bar, Clifford Bar, Derby Bar, to name but a few. Toll houses still exist, recognizable by their angular appearance, so constructed that traffic could be seen from all angles. There is one at Bar Lane, Keighley, another on the borders of Walsden village and another near Bramhope. On the main road between Keighley and Skipton – the Keighley to Kendal turnpike road – there is a horse-trough on which is carved K & K T– R 1825' (Keighley and Kendal Turnpike Road 1825).

Road improvement meant that industrial raw materials and finished products could be moved overland by wagons and carts drawn by teams of horses, which were able to carry more than packhorses.

Rivers, however, had been used for the transport of much commercial produce in the packhorse era and before. Most of the major rivers were navigable, but one of the principal snags of course was that they flowed only where nature had ordained. They were subject to the vagaries of the weather – drought and flood – and also to rival users such as mill-owners who built dams, taking the water needed to enable ships to use them. It was only a short step from the schemes of river improvement – deepening and dredging beds and straightening banks – to the idea of building canals.

The River Aire, for instance, was navigable as far as Knottingley, which was the tidal limit. Cloth from West Yorkshire was taken by land to various inland ports such as Knottingley, Tadcaster and Selby but the expansion of the industry in the seventeenth century led West Yorkshire clothiers to press for better transport. Clothiers of Leeds and Wakefield, for instance, wanted to avoid the necessity of sending their goods twenty-two miles by land. There was also a need to expedite the import of raw wool.

Two allied groups of promoters came forward, composed mainly of clothiers from Leeds and Wakefield, and in 1699 an Act was obtained to enable them to make the Calder navigable from Wakefield to its junction with the Aire at Castleford, and the Aire navigable from Leeds to Castleford and onwards from the confluence to a point 3½ miles above Snaith.

The early trade of the canal was principally that of carrying woollen goods which had been made at Leeds, Wakefield, Halifax and Bradford. Small river craft took them to Rawcliffe, where they were trans-shipped to Hull or other seaports on the English coast and eventually sent to Holland, Bremen, Hamburg and the Baltic. Wool and corn were imported by the same route.

In 1740 the clothiers of Halifax, Ripponden and Elland had petitioned for the navigation of the Calder to be extended upwards from the junction with the Aire and Calder at Wakefield to the Hebble and then up the Hebble to Salterhebble Bridge and on to Halifax.

It was not until 1756 that a definite move was made when it was decided to seek an Act to make the Calder navigable from Wakefield to Elland and on to Halifax. One aim of this was to improve the transport of raw wool to Halifax from Lincolnshire, Nottinghamshire and East Anglia, coming by water to Leeds or Wakefield and then by land, a journey of seventeen miles from Leeds and sixteen from Wakefield. It was thought that a canal would also make corn cheaper.

A committee was appointed which approached John Smeaton and asked him to survey the territory. He was at that time too busy with building the Eddystone Lighthouse to be able to oblige. A further invitation the following year met with more success, and Smeaton's report was favourable. Meanwhile the Rochdale merchants, who obtained their wool from the same sources as the Halifax merchants, had also been considering the proposals for this canal, and they proposed that it should be extended as far as Sowerby Bridge. The Halifax committee were in some fear that this new proposal might jeopardize their chances of getting a Bill through. However, their fears were groundless and in 1758 the Bill was successfully amended and an Act passed to make the Calder navigable from Wakefield to Sowerby Bridge and the Hebble Brook to Salterhebble Bridge at a cost of £2,075. John Smeaton was appointed part-time engineer.

The canal was opened in 1770, and in 1774 an Act was obtained for Sir John Ramsden's canal from Huddersfield to join the Calder and Hebble at Cooper Bridge, which was opened in 1776. Huddersfield was later linked by a canal to the Lancashire system, and the Colne valley was converted from a cul-de-sac into a highway between the West Riding and South Lancashire. The canal was opened as far as Marsden in 1804 and was carried to Ashton-under-Lyne by 1811. The two canals, of course, linked the Aire and Calder system to the Lancashire system.

In March 1792 came a proposal for a canal from Sowerby Bridge to Manchester which, on the third attempt, succeeded in obtaining authorization. It was opened throughout in 1804, providing the first through route across the Pennines, linking Yorkshire to Lancashire with its thirty-five miles of main line and branches. The merchants of Leeds had not been idle in attempting to improve transport in another direction, and in 1770 an Act was obtained for a canal from Leeds to Liverpool. The authorized capital was £260,000 with power to raise an additional £60,000 worth if necessary, and the planned line was 108¾ miles long.[1] Before building was started, there was argument between the merchants of Yorkshire and those of Lancashire. The Yorkshire promoters wanted a direct and cheap communication with Liverpool, while those in Lancashire wanted a less direct line that would include more Lancashire towns. Yorkshire wishes carried the day.

At last, in 1816, forty-six years after the authorization of the canal, it was opened, having cost £1,200,000 and increased in length to 127 miles.[2] Although it was designed for the through carriage of goods, its revenue came principally from the separate trade of the two sides.

Turnpike trusts initially aroused opposition from those who resented paying toll, and the early canals too were opposed. Landowners feared the flooding of good farm land and had serious doubts that the navvies who worked on canal construction, and later the boatmen who operated the boats, would respect the Game Laws. The local population were afraid that local produce would be sent to distant markets to their detriment, and mill-owners feared loss of water from their mill-streams to the canals. Turnpike trustees thought that the tolls on their roads would be reduced.

In West Yorkshire the cutting of the Aire and Calder canal preceded the turnpiking of roads. It was not until 1735 that Yorkshire's first Turnpike Act was passed, authorizing the turnpiking of the road from Rochdale via Blackstone Edge to Halifax and Elland. In 1740 Bills were promoted to turnpike the roads from Halifax via Bradford and Leeds to Selby, from Halifax to Wakefield and from Elland to Leeds. The aims of these proposals were to get the Aire and Calder Canal Company to reduce its toll and to make sure that any future promoters of a navigation of the Calder from Wakefield up to Elland and Halifax would respect the competition of the roads.

Canals provided employment for a great many people. Hundreds of navvies worked on their construction, many more over the years on their maintenance and operating the carrying trade on them; lock-keepers were kept, of course, to help boats through the locks, and maintenance work had to be carried on – masons, bank fencers, painters and blacksmiths were employed in addition to sawyers and labourers. The type of work to be done was varied: ponds and feeder streams had to be dredged and kept free of rubbish; cogs, chains and rollers for lock gates had to be kept in good repair, and so had the sluice gates. Often in winter the canals were covered with ice, and boats were used as ice-breakers; of course the men had to be supplied with special tools to do this.

In 1841 a mason's pay on the Calder and Hebble Navigation varied between 2s. 8d. and 3s. per day, a painter got 3s. 8d., blacksmiths 2s. 6d. to 4s. 6d., bank fencers 2s. to 3s. and lock-keepers 3s. to 3s. 8d. Some canal companies were themselves also boat-operators: in 1887 the Rochdale Canal Company bought its own fleet of boats. Colliery companies and coal-owners also owned quite large fleets of boats, while some operators owned quite small fleets. Facilities varied between the different companies: on some wharves loading and unloading facilities were free, and those wharves seethed with craft jostling to find space to unload. The trader operating in a big way was here at an advantage over his small rival, as those operating large concerns could afford to build their own wharves. He was also at a distinct advantage in the matter of credit. The operator owning a single boat had to trust the boatman with the money to pay his tolls whereas the larger operator paid a lump sum periodically.

One of the first carriers on the Rochdale Canal was Thomas Carver of Halifax who began, about 1808, operating from Dale Street, Manchester. T. and M. Pickford soon started operations with a fleet of fly boats and a warehouse. Albert Wood of Sowerby Bridge had a very large fleet, over forty boats, which were painted in yellow, green and red. All sorts of craft sailed on the Rochdale Canal, packet boats, narrow boats, Humber keels and small coastal craft, and Wood's fleet consisted of flats, keels and narrowboats. In 1912 the weekly wages were: the captain, 15s., mate, 12s. 6d., and driver 12s. 6d. plus tonnage money, which varied from ½d to 6d. Carrying capacity was large, the flats having a capacity of seventy tons, the Yorkshire keels also seventy though they were limited to sixty on the Rochdale Canal, while the narrow boats had a capacity of twenty-five tons. These boats were ideal for the bulk transport of corn, wool, cotton, cattle fodder and stone, and there was flexibility as the different types of boats had different carrying capacities. But transport by canal was slow: the packet boats took seven hours to travel between Rochdale and Manchester and had to negotiate forty-one locks. Pickford's night service took nine hours from

Manchester to Littleborough and twelve hours to Todmorden, and there were frequent queues of vessels to go through the locks.

Recruitment of boatmen was casual in the early days and was possibly on a part-time basis, the boatmen being farmers. In those days distances were short, and the fact that boats had no cabins was of little consequence. If the boatman got cramp, he could get off and walk along the towpath. But as the canal network widened and the distances lengthened, it was necessary for the boatmen to spend a night away from home. They first spent the night at canal-side inns, but as time went on, boats with cabins became more common. The early boatmen were reasonably well paid, £2. 1s. 10d. being an average amount. Out of this a man would have to pay an assistant and provide his own horse, 10s. being a fair price for the expense of a horse and 9s. for an assistant, so his real earnings would be £1. 2s. 10d. a week.

As longer and longer periods of time were spent away from home, boats needed provisions: a sack of potatoes, a quantity of tea and several pounds of meat (boiled before starting off so that it would not go bad). Large loaves of bread could be obtained *en route*, and water was carried in barrels.

But, as more and more men spent more and more time away from home, family boats became increasingly common. It was expensive to maintain two homes – a house and a boat; men missed their womenfolk, women missed husbands and children fathers. Boat families had a special temperament, like gypsies, enjoying the nomadic life and developing a culture of their own with distinctive bright and highly decorated kitchen and household utensils.

Collieries had for some time constructed iron tracks on which their trucks of coal were taken from the pit head to the waterway, a method particularly common on Tyneside, whereas at Middleton Colliery near Leeds, horses and carts were used. In 1749 the estates and collieries at Middleton were inherited by Charles Brandling who, in 1755 made a wagonway from Middleton Colliery to the River Aire and later obtained an Act to enable him to extend it to near Leeds Bridge.

Experiments were progressing with steam locomotives, and

as early as 1804 Richard Trevithick, a Cornishman, invented a locomotive which ran – as an experiment – through London streets to Paddington and Islington and was later put on a railway in South Wales. The enormous increase in the price of all types of corn meant that to keep horses was becoming an expensive luxury, so efforts to find alternative means of transport were redoubled, in much the same way as modern increases in petrol prices cause people to experiment with different means of powering motor cars.

In 1808 John Blenkinsop was appointed agent at Middleton, and he experimented with the steam locomotive, but it was an engineering genius, Matthew Murray, who put Blenkinsop's ideas into practice and succeeded in building a locomotive which worked. This took place in August 1812, after which time it was in daily use, although the opening of the Stockton to Darlington line and the Liverpool to Manchester line have somewhat overshadowed the achievement of Matthew Murray.

Murray had come to Leeds as a penniless young man from his native Stockton on Tees. He had married before he began to earn a journeyman's wages and, being unable to obtain employment, made up his mind to try his luck further south. Lacking even the money necessary for his coach fare or for the boat which would have taken him from the Tees to the Aire, he walked down the Great North Road. He arrived at an inn named the 'Bay Horse', exhausted in body and spirit, and, appealing to the generosity of the landlord, explained his position and offered to repay his account in full at some future date. He managed to get a job with John Marshall, who had recently opened an establishment for the manufacture of flax. Something about Murray's frank, open face must have appealed to Marshall, and he was not disappointed, as the new recruit, turning his attention to the machinery, was able almost at once to suggest improvements and modifications. He was made principal mechanic in the workshop within quite a short time of joining the firm.

In the meantime he had made up his mind to settle in Leeds, so he sent for his wife and rented a cottage in which to live. Continuing as he had begun, he added adaptations of his own to the machinery in his care, improving on the inventions of others

and substituting inexpensive and simple processes in the spinning department in place of costly ones.

In time the mill at Adel became too small, and the works were
moved to Holbeck. In time too Matthew Murray decided he
would do better working for himself and so, in 1795, went into
partnership with James Fenton and David Wood. They established an engineering and machine-making factory in Holbeck,
Wood and Murray being the working partners. So successful
was the business that orders came from all parts, and the
interest, if not the envy, of the firm of Boulton & Watt was
aroused. Mr Murdoch, from the firm of Boulton & Watt, visited
the firm in Leeds and was shown round by Murray, who was
quite open and frank – as was his nature – about all that went on
there, and showed his visitor all the departments. A short time
after Murdoch had returned to Birmingham, a large tract of
land adjoining the firm of Fenton, Wood & Murray was bought
on behalf of Boulton & Watt, thus preventing any expansion of
the firm, now evidently regarded as a rival.

Murray moved his house to Holbeck, improving his dwelling
as he improved everything else in which he was interested: he
introduced some heating apparatus which earned for his house
the name of 'Steam Hall'. There, one evening, came a group of
Luddites threatening destruction to the building and injury to
the inmates unless Murray would promise to cease turning out
the inventions which, as they thought, would threaten their
livelihood. Murray was not at home, but his wife was. Hearing
the angry threats, she calmly replied that she was able to defend
herself and, seizing a pistol, fired it into the crowd. No one was
hurt but they took fright at the pistol shot and fled into the
night.

Murray's work on locomotives did not interrupt his other
work on different kinds of machinery; he continued to improve
machines for the manufacture of flax and was presented with
the gold medal of the Society of Arts for a heckling machine – a
machine for combing flax – which he patented. There is now a
perpetual memorial to him in Leeds, the Matthew Murray
Comprehensive School.

The railway era had arrived, and in West Yorkshire as
elsewhere there were many groups of promoters anxious to

build railways. As many as fifty companies built railways
throughout the county during the nineteenth century, many of
them in the 1840s; and before the end of the century there was a
comprehensive network linking the main towns with each other
and with other towns in adjacent counties as well as centres of
population in other parts of Britain.

In 1834 the first passenger train ran from Leeds to Selby, and
the canal journey of 29½ miles was cut to 20, the result of this
being that the Aire and Calder Canal Company reduced its tolls
considerably. During its first year the railway carried an average of 3,500 passengers a week as compared with an average of
400 on the stage-coaches. In 1840 the public opening of the
North Midlands Railway to Leeds meant that it was now possible to go from Leeds to London in a day, while the following
year trains of the Manchester and Leeds Railway began to run
between those cities. In 1847 a line was opened up Airedale as
far as Keighley, and a few months later a single line extended to
Skipton – which was made into double track by the end of the
year. Eventually a residential express train carried Bradford
wool magnates home from Bradford to Morecambe – the well-
known 'resi', which ran for many years.

Lower Wharfedale, being less industrialized, was in no hurry
to acquire railways but in 1865 passenger trains began running
from Otley to Arthington Junction and also to Ilkley from
Bradford and Leeds. As a result the population of Otley rose
sharply and Ilkley grew from a village to a health and holiday
resort. The improved transport facilities enabled more people
more easily to avail themselves of the water, which had been
found to contain sulphur suitable for curing certain skin diseases. Ilkley also became a dormitory town for Leeds and
Bradford merchants.

A line between Normanton and Hebden Bridge was opened in
1840, and in 1841 the great Summit tunnel between Todmorden
and Littleborough was opened, having taken three years to
build and cost nine lives and £251,000, and forming the last link
in the line across the Pennines between Leeds and Manchester.
When the line was operational, the travelling time from Leeds
to Manchester dropped from 6½ to 2¾ hours.

Another connection was made between Yorkshire and Lanca-

shire when a line was opened between Huddersfield and Manchester. Originally a suggestion had been made to fill in the
canal and use the tunnel for a railway, but the canal company
rejected this offer and decided to sell out to the railway company.
It was agreed that the proposed line should be built on a course
approximately parallel to that of the canal as by this method the
existing tunnel would enable estimates to be more accurate; the
old shafts could be used and barges could remove earth. The
contractor of the tunnel was Thomas Nicolson, so it was known
as Nicolson Tunnel. It cost £201,608, provided employment for
almost 2,000 men at the height of constructional operations and
used over 150,000 pounds of candles at a cost of £3,618.

A traveller to the Huddersfield area was greatly impressed
with the canal tunnel, describing it as being 'put through the
middle of a solid mountain'. It seemed to him all the more
remarkable when the topography of the area would appear to
offer defiance to such an undertaking. He worked out the cost as
£1. 5s. 3⅓d. per inch. The tunnel (connecting Sir John Ramsden's Canal with another to Manchester) was too narrow to
allow boats to pass in it and, in order that boats should not meet
midway, a strict timetable was adhered to. The system of
'legging' was used – common on other canals, notably at Foul-
ridge on the Leeds and Liverpool, whereby the horses were led
over the ground and the boats were 'legged' through the tunnel,
the bargees lying on the boat and working it through by means
of their legs pushing against the wall: '. . . two leggers in each
boat lying on their sides back to back derive a purchase from
shoulder to shoulder, and use their feet against the opposite
walls. It is a hard service, performed in total darkness, and not
altogether void of danger, as the roof is composed of loose
material.'[3] The leggers were casual workers hired for that
particular purpose who stayed a few days or a few weeks and
then departed for a change of occupation. The towing horses
were sent over the hill in charge of a man who was paid 6d. for
conducting each horse, so presumably this was also casual
labour.

Although the post-war era has seen a decline in the canals and
the demise of many railways in the county, there is still a
network of canals. The Aire and Calder is constantly being

improved by the British Waterways Board and is used by freight traffic, oil-tankers and coal-boats, for example, when taking coal to power stations. The Aire and Calder meets the Leeds and Liverpool canal at Leeds and also, in the west, leads into the Calder and Hebble, while the southern part is the route to the Sheffield and South Yorkshire Navigation. The Calder and Hebble is navigable from Wakefield as far as Sowerby Bridge where it joins the Rochdale Canal, unfortunately not now navigable, parts of it in West Yorkshire having been covered by roads so that now there is no through route. Sir John Ramsden's Canal is known now as Huddersfield Broad Canal, and the 3¼ miles from Cooper Bridge – its junction with the Aire and Calder – to Apsley Base Huddersfield, is navigable. The Huddersfield Narrow Canal – the section from Huddersfield along the Colne Valley to Standedge Tunnel – is at present closed to navigation, although the Huddersfield Canal Society is campaigning for the canal and tunnel to be re-opened. The entire length of the Leeds and Liverpool Canal is navigable.

There is still a network of railways serving the county, with regular services running across the Pennines to Manchester via Huddersfield and the Colne Valley and also via Halifax and the Calder Valley. Trains run through Airedale from Leeds and on to Morecambe and also to Carlisle, and there is a service up Wharfedale to Ilkley. South, there is a connection to Wakefield and Doncaster and on to London, and east to York and Scarborough, Selby and Hull, and there is also a line to York from Leeds via Harrogate. Trains also operate between Huddersfield and Sheffield.

In spite of the fact that we are told repeatedly by printed and verbal propaganda that this is the age of the train, trends and events seem to indicate that it is in fact the age of the road. A considerable amount of air space has been devoted by local radio to accounts of projected new motorways and reports of public enquiries and continues to be devoted, especially in winter, to reports of weather conditions on existing motorways. One of these is, of course, the M1, part of which goes through West Yorkshire, while its other major road is the M62 which crosses the Pennines.

Fog and snow are, and always have been, a winter hazard in

the north of England, particularly on the Pennines. Any road crossing this hill range would be subject to these elements, but the plan of the M62 meant that the road would for much of its length exceed 1,000 feet and reach a maximum height of 1,220 feet. It was intended that it should be in use for twenty-four hours a day, 365 days a year, and so it was imperative that some method should be found of keeping the road free from snow and ice. The original intention was to put electrically heated cables under all that part of the carriageway exceeding a height of 750 feet but, because of very high cost, this idea was abandoned. It was then decided that the road should be designed in such a way that any falling snow should be blown off the carriageway. Exhaustive tests were made in the National Physical Laboratory in which powdered Balsa wood was used as artificial snow. This was blown into model cuttings, and as a result of these experiments it was eventually decided to 'step' them, thereby encouraging snowdrifts to form on the steps rather than on the carriageway.

In 1961 the Minister of Transport asked the County Councils of Lancashire and the West Riding of Yorkshire to recommend a route for a motorway across the Pennines. Three years later the line of the route was settled, in May 1968 work on the motorway started, and in October 1971 the Queen officially inaugurated the Pennine section.

Considerable engineering skill has gone into the building of the road, especially some of the highest parts. The Deanhead cutting, which is 180 feet deep – the deepest road cutting in the country, and the building of the Scammonden Dam, for example, entailed great technical ingenuity. The Scammonden Dam, which took over three years to build, fits well into its surroundings – a landscape consultant was employed in connection with its construction. Trees have been planted and parking facilities built, and the whole area forms a leisure complex, a sailing club using the reservoir. Landscaping along the verges of the motorway helps to make it a pleasant thoroughfare, and some of the bridges crossing the motorway are graceful and attractive.

5

Markets

Probably as early as the eleventh century most towns had markets, which were originally held on a Sunday in or near the churchyard. The market in Keighley was held on Church Green for five centuries, very near the churchyard but never inside it, but was never held on a Sunday, unlike Bradford which did hold a Sunday market. To the medieval mind there was nothing incongruous about holding a market on a Sunday or siting it in or near church premises. Religion and business were at that time linked; representatives of the church and of great monasteries attended fairs; indeed, they could not have existed without replenishing their stocks of provisions from the great fairs. In fact, many monasteries were themselves owners of markets and fairs. The market and fair at Wetherby, for instance, was in the ownership of the Knights Templars, who were granted permission to hold a market on Thursday of each week and a yearly fair lasting three days.

A contract, when entered into in the presence of a representative of the faith or associated with some tangible manifestation of religion such as the tomb of a saint, or within the sacred precincts of the church, was regarded as solemn and binding and was not, in the Middle Ages, easily set aside.

From a practical point of view, Sunday was a day on which people gathered at church in order to attend Mass; it was therefore more convenient for them to see the goods on sale rather than wait for the merchant to peddle his wares from door to door. Likewise it was easier for the trader to deal with an assembled crowd rather than visit scattered homesteads.

Whilst it was true to say that some came to church and also traded, and that some came to trade and attended church, by the

late twelfth and thirteenth markets were becoming more secu-
lar in character. The ecclesiastical authorities and reformers
discouraged holding markets in churchyards and on Sundays,
and instead they came to be held on weekdays on sites away
from church premises.

In an age when few people could read or write and when
documentation and written records were few, it was important,
as a deterrent to cheating, that all buying and selling was done
in the open, and this was one of the reasons why in the Middle
Ages, markets were important.

To the person, or body, who owned the right to hold them,
markets were, and were intended to be, profitable ventures. The
king's licence had to be obtained before a market could be held,
and the possession of a market charter was a valued privilege.
During the thirteenth century there were 3,300 grants of markets and fairs, the licence being given only if the institution of a
fair or market did not mean injury to trade elsewhere. It was
usual therefore to grant licences for markets only if they were
about six miles apart.

The tolls levied were a valued item of the revenue of a king
and, subsequently, of whoever was granted the charter. Many
towns were walled and traders entered by one of the gates,
which made it easy to collect the toll they were required to pay
on the goods they brought to sell; they also paid toll on the stalls
they used or the space they occupied. In Wakefield, aliens,
meaning anyone who was not a citizen of Wakefield, paid ½d. on
every load of corn or grain, although the people of the town or
parish were exempt. Tolls charged to aliens on cloth were as
follows: for every pack of Yorkshire broadcloth, 8d.; every pack
of narrow cloth 4d.; every pack of Kendal cloth 1d.; and every
pack of Lancashire cloth 1d. or 2d. At Adwalton Fair there was a
toll of 1d. for every lamb bought or sold and likewise for every
live sheep bought or sold.

Such was the prosperity of thirteenth-century Wakefield that
the traders round the market-place needed to enlarge their
stalls. In 1295 Robert Kaye paid 6d. to enlarge his booth by three
feet and agreed to pay another 6d. for the concession and ½d.
increase in his annual rent. John Cussyng wanted to lengthen
his booths towards the north in 1297, for which he paid 12d.,

with an extra rent of 3d., and he paid the same price for an extension towards the south.

In return for the tolls, the owner of the market was expected to provide certain guarantees. Merchants had a right to look to him for protection and for peace during the time the market was in progress, and he was also responsible for the provision of justice. Thus no buying or selling could be done until the market bell had sounded. The court of pie-powder, thought to be a corruption of the words '*pieds poudreux*', 'dusty feet' (many of the merchants who came to trade would have dusty feet from tramping along unmetalled roads), was the place where disputes between buyer and seller were settled. The jury was chosen from a group of traders at the fair. An incident at Lee Fair, which must have been a common type of occurrence, illustrates the sort of case the court of pie-powder would be called upon to deal with. A certain John de Heton had overturned a stall; what occasioned this we are not told; whether it was after an argument with the stallholder about the price he was being asked to pay, or whether he was drunk, we do not know. As a result the stallholder lost twenty gallons of beer worth 2s. 4d. a cask, valued at 12d. and a sack, worth 8d., the covering of his stall was also torn, the damage amounting to 12d., and he suffered other (unspecified) injuries, in all amounting to 40s.

Weights and measures were local and varied between one county and another; coinage too varied and the reluctance of some kings to come to grips with the necessity of issuing a standard coinage caused confusion. The maintenance of an acceptable standard both of coinage and of weights and measures throughout the country was the business of royal officers under the authority of the royal Clerk of the Market.

Marketing was dominated by the medieval theory of the just price, an amount whereby all who contributed to the production and sale of the article could make an honest living and a modest profit. The idea that prices were ruled by the law of supply and demand, or more particularly that artificial scarcity could be created and the price of an article thus inflated, was abhorrent to the medieval mind. Cheating was a relatively minor offence; it could in any case be detected and minimized by an elaborate system of checking. But to try to corner (forestall) the market by buying supplies before they reached it, or to purchase (regrate) large quantities of goods to re-sell at a higher price, was regarded as a heinous crime. Medieval traders were no more honest than many of their modern counterparts, and the temptation to indulge in these sharp practices must have been great. The prevention, detection and punishment of such crimes was the prerogative of the State rather than the owner of the market.

A weekly market was the trading territory of people in a locality many of whom came from the surrounding villages to sell their surplus produce. Similar in structure, although longer lasting and less frequent, was the fair, primarily a gathering for trading and not for pleasure and entertainment. Fairs, like markets, were originally held near to a church and they lasted several days, originating at a time when there was likely to be a gathering of people, for example the saint's day of the local church. To fairs came not only local merchants but also those from further afield.

Fairs were often held for the purpose of trading in some specific commodity or commodities, although this would not exclude the presence there of merchants trading in a wide variety of other goods. Many fairs in West Yorkshire were for the sale of animals, horned cattle, sheep, hogs, horses. Bingley was granted a licence for the sale of horned cattle, sheep and linen, Bradford horned cattle and household furniture with another fair for hogs. Huddersfield Fair was for the sale of lean horned cattle and horses, Keighley for horned cattle, brass, pewter and pedlary, Lee for horses and cheese – an ill-assorted combination. Wakefield had a licence for pleasure fairs and toys. Adwalton was granted a licence for a fair for the sale of horses, sheep, pedlary and tinware.

Stolen goods were often offered for sale at fairs, and among the items thus disposed of were horses, which were especially valuable. It was very difficult to identify stolen animals, to trace the thieves and bring them to justice, so an Act, passed in 1555 to try to stop this traffic in stolen goods, gave rise to horse fairs being held independently of other fairs. The Act said that whoever took the tolls had to record in his entry the colour of each horse which was sold or exchanged and at least one distinguishing mark by which it could be identified.

A subsequent Act, passed in 1589, stated that no sale of a horse was legal unless certain conditions had been satisfied: the animal was to be put on view to the public for at least an hour between sunrise and sunset, and the toll-taker had to be able to identify the vendor or, alternatively, a guarantee of his honesty must be provided by 'one sufficient and credible' person. Entry must be made of the names of the vendors and buyers, and a note made of the vouchers and prices paid.

Adwalton, which had a horse fair, was ideally placed for such an event. Situated roughly midway between Bradford and Morley and between Halifax and Leeds, it lies within easy reach of places which were centres of the woollen industry, and places where other markets were held.

The Book of Sales of 1631 indicates brisk business, with trading coming from all over the county of Yorkshire as well as from Derbyshire, Lancashire, Cumberland and Westmorland. The entries in the book complied with the terms of the Act, so there were such entries as 'One blacke fillie slitt in both eares . . .' and 'One gray fillie with a white starre . . .'. Each description was followed by the words 'trots unto' and the name of the new owner, evoking a picture of a horse hopefully and joyfully entering upon a new and happy partnership with a fresh master.

The serious side of trading was apparent at a horse fair. The traders, who included clothiers, yeomen, chapmen, a card-maker, a tanner and a shoemaker, would need a horse to conduct business in much the same way as a doctor nowadays needs a motor car. To go to the horse fair, therefore, would be a matter of business, although there would be a great deal of pleasure involved – meeting old acquaintances, making new friends, exchanging gossip.

Lee Fair was another fair of great importance in the past. It was held at West Ardsley near Wakefield and the reason for its being known as Lee Fair is somewhat obscure but possibly originated from a Dr Legh who had connections with West Ardsley. A century ago it was important for the horse fairs which were held there. There were two, known as 't' first Lee' and 't' latter Lee', held respectively on 24 August and 17

September. In the eighteenth century there was one fair which lasted three weeks and which was a market-place for the sale of nearly all kinds of produce. It was one of the most important fairs in the kingdom and attracted local tradesmen who used it as a sort of wholesale market, storing their produce in barns and selling it later. 'Multitudes came from towards Huddersfield and many other parts of the county.' It also attracted merchants from overseas – from France, Spain, Florence, the Low Countries and Germany. The fair seems to have fulfilled the function of Yorkshire's answer to Gretna Green as it was customary for a priest and clerk to be ready at all times of the day during the fair to marry anyone who so wished, in the church.

There must have been many more fairs of a local nature. One such was a cattle fair held high on the hills above Cornholme in the Cliviger Valley at the end of April each year, with another three weeks later. The cattle were driven on foot from the surrounding areas, and the fair took up the whole road. When the animals had been sold, they were put into a field until the farmer had got his full complement, when they were driven off along the roads in much the same way as they had arrived. Every man did his own bargaining, and the sale was sealed with a handslap. It was customary for the seller to give to the buyer a small proportion of the sale money as a token of luck.

There were several places in the county, of which Pontefract was one, which had a charter for a cloth fair. During the seventeenth century there was an expansion in the woollen industry, and several towns applied for licences to have weekly cloth markets, which was not very popular in those towns which had cloth fairs. The application of Wakefield for a weekly cloth market was counter-petitioned unsuccessfully by Barnsley, while Huddersfield applied for a charter for a weekly cloth market in 1671. These markets were held out of doors. Huddersfield merchants, for example, displayed their cloth for sale on the walls of the churchyard. Leeds cloth market was held on the narrow bridge which crossed the River Aire at the bottom of Briggate, but was found, in the course of time, to block the way of passers-by and vehicles coming into the town centre and in 1684 was moved higher up Briggate, where markets took place on Tuesdays and Saturdays.

The new market in Briggate aroused the interest of Defoe:

Early in the morning, trestles are placed in two rows in the street . . ., across which boards are laid, which make a kind of temporary counter on either side from one end of the street to the other. The clothiers come early in the morning with their cloth, and . . . few bring more than one piece . . .
   . . . about six o'clock in summer and seven in winter, the clothiers all being come by that time, the market bell at the old chapel by the bridge rings . . .
   In a little less than an hour all the business is done, in less than half an hour you will perceive the cloth begin to move off . . .[1]

During the eighteenth century cloth halls were built in many of the West Yorkshire towns to provide better marketing facilities for the buyers and sellers in the rapidly expanding cloth industry. But there was a great deal of – not very friendly – rivalry and a distinct element of 'keeping up with the Joneses' about the building of cloth halls.

Halifax was the first town to have its own cloth hall, during the seventeenth century. A bid to be second in the field came from an unexpected quarter. In 1709 the lords of the manor of Hightown and Liversedge petitioned Queen Anne for a charter to hold a weekly cloth market on a Monday, i.e. the day before Leeds. The Sheriff held an enquiry and it was decided that a market at Hightown for white woollen cloth would be detrimental and prejudicial to the markets at Leeds, Huddersfield, Halifax and Wakefield. Hightown renewed its petition but was again unsuccessful.

In 1710 Wakefield acquired a cloth hall, an event which piqued the merchants of Leeds, who were determined not to be outdone by Wakefield. In August 1710 Ralph Thoresby, the Leeds historian, wrote in his diary: '. . . rode with the Mayor . . . and others to my Lord Irwin's at Temple Newsam, about the erection of a hall for white cloths in Kirkgate, to prevent the damage to this town . . . of one lately erected at Wakefield, with design to engross the woollen trade.'[2]

In April 1711 the Leeds White Cloth Hall in Kirkgate was opened and the trade in white cloths flourished to such an extent that this hall became too small and in 1755 a second White Cloth Hall was opened. This was on a site south of Leeds Bridge between Hunslet Lane and Meadow Lane, and in time trade outgrew the capacity even of this hall to contain it so that in twenty years the possibility of opening yet another hall was being considered. The factor which impelled merchants to do something positive about a new hall was similar to that which had galvanized them into action in the first place.

Competition from a smaller rival, this time Gomersal, was the cause. Gomersal was in the heart of the white cloth area, and the merchants and landed gentry wanted a hall of their own to save the clothiers the hassle of the journey to Leeds and back. A piece of land was given and money subscribed. The Leeds Cloth Hall Trustees meanwhile devoted a great deal of time and effort to trying to scotch the idea, pointing out that the erection of a cloth hall was illegal without a licence from the Crown. However, the Gomersal hall was built and survived for about thirty years, never succeeding in seriously injuring the trade at the Leeds Cloth Hall. A third cloth hall, much bigger than either of its predecessors, was opened in Leeds in 1775.

Even after the opening of the first White Cloth Hall there was considerable trade still in Briggate in coloured cloths. However, in 1755 Leeds obtained an Improvement Act which provided for the widening of Briggate, which would not only have entailed disturbance to the coloured cloth stalls but, as if to add insult to injury, caused the stallholders to be charged increased fees to help to defray the cost of improvements. In 1756 clothiers began to discuss the possibility of opening a hall for the sale of coloured cloths and eventually acquired a site somewhere near the present GPO. In 1766 a cloth hall was built in Huddersfield which was enlarged in 1780, and in 1766 also a Tammy Hall was built in Wakefield for the sale of worsteds.

As early as the seventeenth century a specialized building had existed in Halifax known as the Cloth Hall. By the beginning of the eighteenth century it was in a poor state of repair, and in 1708 three local gentlemen were permitted by Lord Ingram, the Lord of the Manor of Halifax, to renovate it.

During the eighteenth century trade at Halifax, as elsewhere in West Yorkshire, increased and by the beginning of the 1770s local manufacturers were selling their wares in the open, so dissatisfied had they become with the existing building. Knowing of the cloth halls which had been built elsewhere, in neighbouring towns, and feeling that they must 'keep up with the neighbours', some manufacturers and buyers put an advertisement in the *Leeds Mercury* on 5 April 1774 which gave notice of a public meeting on 9 April to consider opening subscriptions for the building of a new piece hall in Halifax.

The building was opened, amid great pomp and ceremony, in January 1779, having cost £8,460. 18s. 9½d. The most contemporary description available, written about a century later, describes great rejoicing. People came in from the surrounding villages, and many of the houses in the town sported new paint. Workmen in various trades assembled with their masters and marched to the Piece Hall, the wool-combers wearing three-cornered hats, wigs, long coats, breeches and buckled shoes with coloured shoulder sashes.

Bradford was late in acquiring a piece hall. This was because worsted manufacture which was based in there was more capitalized than woollen manufacture; there were consequently fewer manufacturers, individual stocks were larger, and there was considerably more direct dealing. Those worsted manufacturers who lived in Bradford had piece rooms at their own houses, and those who came from outside had cubicles in a large room at the 'White Lion', in Kirkgate. This was not a satisfactory arrangement, and in 1773 a cloth hall was opened which had a hundred apartments; but with expanding trade this was soon found to be too small, and in 1780 it was extended to provide accommodation for another 158 merchants. The hall was essentially for the sale of worsted, but provision was made at the conclusion of the cloth market for the sale of yarn.

The cloth halls showed certain similarities but there were also some differences. The third White Cloth Hall in Leeds was arranged round a quadrangle, and the interior was divided into five long streets down each side of which ran the rows of stalls, in all 1,213 stalls. The Halifax Piece Hall is a rectangular building round which is a colonnade on each side, and in each colonnade small rooms, 315 in all. Thus the clothiers of Halifax were able, as those who traded in Leeds and Huddersfield were not, to leave their pieces in a room from one market day to the next. On the west side there is a ground floor and one upper storey, whereas the east side has a ground floor and two upper storeys. The Huddersfield Cloth Hall, two storeys high, was circular and subdivided into streets.

The terms of letting differed. The clothiers at the Leeds White Cloth Hall of 1775 acquired the freehold of their stalls by payments of 30s. plus a small annual fee to defray the cost of cleaning, repairs and so on. At the coloured Cloth Hall a clothier seems to have received a stall for every £2. 10s. he subscribed, but no one had more than three. At the Halifax Piece Hall the original subscribers to its building were given the first chance of the rooms at an annual rent of roughly £28, while the small weaver was given the opportunity, for a small fee, to display his goods on the grass in the centre. At the Huddersfield Cloth Hall there were no regulations about clothiers having served an apprenticeship before being qualified to use the hall; any weaver could come and sell his goods provided he paid toll.

Management differed: the Leeds Cloth Halls were under the management of fifteen trustees, the Halifax Piece Hall under a committee, whereas the Huddersfield Cloth Hall was managed by Sir John Ramsden, who had built it.

A feature of all the halls was a cupola from which a bell announced the commencement of trading, and in all cases no one might trade until the bell rang. It was rung again to warn traders of the approaching end of the market, and again at the end, and anyone continuing trading after the final bell had rung was fined. Traders of varying degrees of prosperity came to markets and subsequently to the halls; some came carrying pieces on their own heads and shoulders, some brought them on the backs of horses, while others, the more substantial clothiers, had horses and carts. They came from long distances to the Halifax Piece Hall – for instance, from Burnley, Bingley, Colne, Skipton, Haworth, Keighley and Bradford. Most would have had an early start, and all would need refreshment before they left for home again. Briggate, the venue of the Leeds market before the opening of the cloth halls, was well provided with inns, which supplied a clothier's twopennyworth or Brigg-shot. This was a pot of ale, a noggin of pottage and a trencher of boiled or roast beef, price 2d. The innkeepers in the early years of the eighteenth century tried to get the stalls in their own hands so that they could compel the clothiers who wished to use them to patronize their particular inns or pay an exorbitant fee. However, the City Fathers stepped in, decreeing that from Lady Day (25 March) to Michaelmas (29 September) no stall was to be set up before four o'clock in the morning, and from Michaelmas to Lady Day not before six in the morning.

If one stands for ten minutes in any one of many West Yorkshire markets and uses a little imagination, one can picture the market scene in the Middle Ages. A market had colour and life and bustle, and for someone on an isolated farm or in a small village community the long trudge to and from the nearest market was a small price to pay for the rich return in human contact, exchange of ideas, local gossip. One can imagine the farmers and villagers plodding back across the country footpaths carrying their loads, their hearts lightened and their spirits lifted by contact with friends.

The rarer fair on the other hand must have been a great event, to be anticipated with great excitement and talked about until the next fair. It was a rowdy affair with the mingled shouts of the traders advertising their wares, the bleating of sheep and goats, the lowing of cattle, the cackle of hens, the shrill voices of children and the babble of adult voices and perhaps above all that the screech of some exotic bird. Tinkers sold pans and cauldrons, potters pots and jars; there were baskets for sale and woven mats. A potpourri of smells assailed the nostrils as merchants sold ginger, nutmeg, pepper, cloves and cinnamon, and more homely smells as stalls and cookshops sold pies. There was a blaze of colour from the bright silks, carpets and jewels from the East. Quack doctors wheedled pennies from people on the pretext of curing toothache and sold linctus as a cure-all for every ache and pain. There was free entertainment as well, for one could gape at the unfortunates who had been put in the stocks or pillory for fraudulent trading.

On St Bartholemew's Day, when Lee Fair ended, it was usual for scholars from the grammar schools of Leeds, Wakefield and other places to be brought to the fair for disputation or to make sure that their standard of classical learning was high enough.

This must have been highly entertaining for the onlookers –
even though perhaps the proceeding was too intellectual for
many – as they were keen to join in from time to time.

Only names remain to recall former days in markets and
fairs; the Shambles, Cornmarket, Shoemarket and Horsefair
remind us of the practice of selling the same sort of goods in the
same place, for stalls selling one commodity were located in
rows. Few modern markets keep to this custom; Leeds does, in
Butchers' Row and Game Row.

Some of West Yorkshire's markets are a pleasure to visit. In
the traditional market towns where there is a market-place,
this is a focal point, whereas the newer industrial towns have
had to find space where they can. In Wetherby the market stalls
cluster round the town hall, and in Pontefract and Otley they
are grouped round the old market cross and hall, spilling over
into the streets. In Pontefract some of the stalls back onto the
parish church, and the situation with the market cross and
church really gives atmosphere, making it perhaps of all the
West Yorkshire markets the most delightful.

The present market cross was built in 1734 although the site
was a focal point for hundreds of years before this. In the Middle
Ages St Oswald's Cross stood there and was regarded as a
sanctuary, giving freedom from arrest by the Corporation, and
the cross also became a meeting-place for the Wapentake of
Osgoldcross, a corruption of St Oswald's Cross. It was also
important as a rendezvous for traders, who found the area round
it a suitable place to display their wares and sell their goods. By
the Norman period a town was well established, with a large
market-place stretching from Beastfair to Woolmarket and
from Cornmarket to Gillygate.

The present cross was given by Mrs Elizabeth Dupier, whose
husband was a member of the garrison of Gibraltar at the time
that it was held by pro-Bourbon forces for King Philip V in the
War of the Spanish Succession. On 3 August 1704 an Anglo-
Dutch force, commanded by Admiral Sir George Rooke and the
Prince of Hesse-Darmstadt, attacked the rock in support of the
rival claimant to the Spanish throne, Archduke Charles of
Austria. The following day the garrison surrendered. It is said
that Dupier was instrumental in bringing about the fall of

Gibraltar to Sir George Rooke and that he received a pension for his services.

The buttercross is an attractive focal point for the market and was used earlier this century by farmers' wives who brought in dairy produce to sell, for of course it was the practice, not so long ago, for country people to bring in surplus home-grown produce for sale. The markets where this is still the case are few and far between; York, Kendal and Carlisle come to mind. Modern markets thrive on mass-produced goods and chain-store seconds.

Some towns established reputations for the sale of commodities on a larger scale. Wakefield, for instance, was important for the sale of corn, and so was Otley, which supplied corn to the manufacturing districts as well as supplying the butchers of Leeds with cattle, sheep and calves. Huddersfield had an important pig market which was supplied almost exclusively from Ireland, the pigs coming by sea to Liverpool and then being driven across the Pennines. Immediately before being put on sale the pigs were washed in the river, which must have been pleasantly cooling for them after their long march: 'The herd being driven up to their bellies in the river, one man was entirely occupied in sluicing them with water from a pail . . . Another fellow anointed them one after another with yellow soap, and so soon as he had raised a copious lather rubbed the hide, first soundly with his hands and then with the teeth of a horse-mane comb.'[3] The pig-washing must have been an interesting sight, as interesting as today's washing of horses in the Eden at Appleby during the horse fair, when the traders use Fairy liquid detergent.

The old chartered markets still flourish in West Yorkshire; Otley for instance has been in existence for some thousand years. But the newer towns, Todmorden, Sowerby Bridge and Hebden Bridge, also established markets. In 1802, at a meeting of the parishioners of Todmorden and Walsden in Gauxholme, it was decided to establish a market on Thursdays for the benefit of manufacturers and tradesmen. Later two markets were established, one for corn and provisions on Thursdays and another each Saturday for meat, fish and greengroceries, while a cattle market was held on the first Thursday in each month. Although

the markets were newly established, the townspeople adhered
to the old idea of linking church and Sunday with trading, the
market-place being established at White Hart Fold near St
Mary's Church. Often on a Sunday after morning service the
parish clerk acted as town crier and at the churchyard gate
announced which local farmer or butcher would kill a cow or
sheep that week so that fresh meat could be obtained.

Many modern markets, particularly the old chartered markets, are held in market-places: Otley, Wetherby and Pontefract
come to mind; Sowerby Bridge has a market-place and so does
Batley – a very pleasant one. Other places, Castleford and
Hemsworth for example, have made do with spare ground and
odd corners, while Heckmondwike traders put up stalls in the
streets – and the traffic seems to cope. Wakefield's market,
which seems to take place nearly every day, is very big, while
Dewsbury's is even bigger, and Holmfirth and Huddersfield
tuck their markets away in obscure places – Holmfirth particularly – so that they are difficult for the tourist to locate. For
markets are an attraction to the tourist and casual meanderer
as well as to the serious shopper – 'Try a different market this
week' urges a notice on the buses in the Hemsworth/Pontefract/
Wakefield district.

For tourist attraction the markets at the Piece Hall must
merit the highest rating, for the Piece Hall itself is one of the
greatest attractions the county has to offer, and the impression
made on a visitor going for the first time is very considerable.
Many of the 315 rooms are now let to private traders, almost all
of them selling articles of an 'arty crafty' nature. Some of the
goods are mass produced and the sort one could buy anywhere,
but a great many more are craftsman-made, hand-thrown
pottery, hand knitwear, paintings, woodware and so on. In the
open centre space, markets are held every Friday, Saturday and
Sunday, and controversy is currently raging about what consti-
tutes a souvenir, so that the Sunday trading laws need not be
contravened. Often there is a band playing, there are stalls
selling hot dogs and coffee, and the whole atmosphere is one of
carnival.

In some towns, such as Leeds, Todmorden and Halifax, part of
the market trading is done in covered market halls, while in

Keighley and Bradford the new market halls, which constitute the entire market, have completely destroyed any market atmosphere. Bingley has a very small market while controversy reigns in the town as to whether to bring back the eighteenth-century market hall, buttercross and stocks to the town centre or to leave them where they have been for a long time, in the local park. Bingley's is – arguably – the finest market cross in the county and would provide a splendid focal point for a market.

People shout much less at markets than formerly, although the Leeds greengrocers do so. The most regrettable feature of modern markets is the demise of the pot man with his patter, his wit and repartee and his dexterous and swift handling of his wares. Pot fairs never were a feature of West Yorkshire life as they were, and still are, of Lancashire.

6

Metropolitan Centres

The common denominator linking the five cities at the head of
the West Yorkshire Metropolitan Areas is wool, which has
dominated all aspects of West Yorkshire life for hundreds of
years. In the fifteenth and sixteenth centuries Leeds and
Wakefield were becoming famous as markets and for the homes
of merchants, and by the seventeenth century Wakefield was
the principal wool market of the district, whereas Leeds had
become an important market for cloth. Halifax achieved sup-
remacy in the woollen industry and, by 1750, was the most
important centre for the output of worsteds.

By the first decades of the eighteenth century Bradford's
fortunes were at a low ebb, and although the opinions of Leeds,
Wakefield, Halifax and Huddersfield were heard whenever
petitions about the woollen industry were sent to Parliament,
Bradford was silent. In the last years of the eighteenth century
she began to come to life, for she had industrialists of enterprise
and vigour who experimented with new yarns and machines.
Bradford was linked with the Leeds and Liverpool Canal, giving
greatly improved communication and the coming of the railway
improved communication still further, and so she began to rival
Halifax – which was outside the main thoroughfare of commercial traffic – until Halifax was eventually overtaken by Bradford as the worsted capital.

Standing on the path at Sandal Castle, the seat of government
of the Warenes and later lords in the Middle Ages, one has a
splendid view of the modern seat of government, the City of
Wakefield, headquarters formerly of a third of Yorkshire and
now the chief administrative centre of a smaller county as well
as a Metropolitan Borough. Sandal represented a feudal govern-

ment in which in a sense State and Church were linked. The Wakefield skyline shows an authority both spiritual and temporal; there is the slender, graceful spire of the cathedral which dominates the scene; behind, but not so tall, the clock tower of the town hall and the domed tower of the county hall, and in the foreground the multi-storey office block of a government department.

For a long time the cathedral spire has been a landmark; in the days when there was only Mother Church to give spiritual comfort and practical help to those in distress, and through the days when the growing towns were groping towards full independent self-government.

John Housman, an early nineteenth-century topographer, said, 'The lofty spire of the old church is conspicuous at a great distance.'[1] For of course it *was* the old church; not until 1888 was the Anglican diocese formed and the parish church elevated to the status of a cathedral. And 'old' is the operative word for there was a church on the site in pre-Conquest times which was rebuilt at some time after Domesday, this building later being replaced by a new church of Early English design which was consecrated in 1329 by Archbishop Melton whose statue can be seen at the entrance to the north choir aisle. In the fifteenth century the tower and spire were completed, the spire being 247 feet high, and aisles and clerestory added. In 1905 the extension at the east end was consecrated by Dr Walsham How, who was the first Bishop of Wakefield – famous for his hymn 'For All the Saints'. This extension comprised a new sanctuary, three chapels on its north, east and south sides, with new vestries and a chapter house beneath. The latest addition to the cathedral complex is a Memorial Hall to the late Bishop Eric Treacey which was opened by HRH Princess Margaret in October 1982.

Travellers in the nineteenth century who passed through Wakefield spoke of the streets; one described them as new, another as handsome, another as clean. They would no doubt have been impressed by the pedestrian precinct near the cathedral. It is tolerably new, certainly handsome and, since it is a popular picnicking spot, one hopes it will remain clean. There are seats provided a-plenty, and it is an ideal resting-place for shoppers, for those with nothing much to do who want to feel at the heart of things, for a lunchtime rendezvous for workers in shops and offices, and for school parties who need to rest their weary limbs. The cathedral is certainly in the heart of its town. Most other streets in the shopping centre are nondescript, being very much like the streets of any other large town, with the usual array of shops, although this is not to say that Wakefield is not a good shopping centre.

Past visitors spoke of it as an opulent town with the streets containing 'remarkably handsome and spacious mansion houses built of red brick and stone'.[2] One writer said: '. . . because of greatly improved trade the inhabitants have been able to ornament it [the town] with many respectable houses.'[3]

Some of the most ornamental and respectable houses in the town are to be found when one comes in from the north-east on the Leeds bus route, just wide of the town centre. But by far the most gracious aspect is the approach from the north, where one passes St John's Church, built in the 1790s, with its graveyard, and the streets of superb houses nearby – now in a conservation area. Coming further into the town centre is one of the most handsome and impressive streets in any town in the north of England – Wood Street, also a conservation area; here are the buildings which are at the administrative heart of the county and the borough. One of these buildings is the museum, built in the early 1820s for use as a music saloon and used later as a mechanics' institute. Shares were sold at £20 each in order to raise capital, the interest for the shareholders to come from the rents; in anticipation, a deposit was put on a plot of land which belonged to Reverend William Wood, of Woodthorpe, from whom Wood Street takes its name. Since the summer of 1954 the City Museum has been housed in these premises.

There is also the town hall opened in 1880 by the Mayor, and designed in French Renaissance style with a tower 194 feet high and a clock face on each side. More stately is the county hall: it was in 1894 that the West Riding County Council, having been constituted in 1888, decided to locate its headquarters in Wakefield. It is a handsome building, opened in February 1898 by the Marquess of Ripon: the side facing Bond Street has a series of niches – seven in all – in which at one time were large figures representing the main industries of the West Riding.

They showed a miner – stripped to the waist, an iron-moulder with his tools, a spinner with a shawl, a glass-blower with a pipe, a farm labourer in a smock, an engineer with a cog wheel, and a potter. This seems a comprehensive and unbiased spread, embracing the industrial activities of the county. Should figures occupy the niches again, it is interesting to speculate on what would best represent the county's industries in the 1980s. Mining could be represented, as it was in the nineteenth century, and agriculture and textiles would also have a place, although certainly not showing a farm worker in a smock or a spinner in a shawl. There would be a need also to show the service industries, especially those connected with leisure and transport.

Between the two halls of government stands the distinguished building of the court house, identifiable by its fluted Doric columns.

In Wentworth Street, between the Wood Street buildings and the St John's area, is Wentworth House, an extremely fine Georgian building which was built in 1802–03, bought in 1878 for £8,000 by the Governors of the Queen Elizabeth Grammar School and opened, also in 1878, as Wakefield Girls' High School. It is still used by this school, which has since grown, and extensions have been built.

Queen Elizabeth Grammar School for boys is now housed in handsome premises in Northgate, in a building erected in 1833. The school is, of course, of much older foundation than this, having been founded in 1592 by the Saviles, ancestors of the Earl of Mexborough, '... for the teaching, instructing, and bringing up children and youth in grammar and other good learning.'[4] The headmaster, and probably the second master also, was usually complimented with a small donation at Christmas. The school had several exhibitions and scholarships to the universities of Oxford and Cambridge, three of them of a considerable amount. In 1822 the salary of the headmaster, a reverend gentleman, was £180.

Until about the middle of the eighteenth century, Wakefield was the capital of the West Yorkshire clothing industry, a position achieved because of its situation at the then limit of navigation of the River Calder. It escaped the worst impact of the Industrial Revolution and developed as an agricultural centre, having a corn market, which, handling about 15,000 quarters of grain each week, was one of the largest in the country; the extent of its malt market was almost as great.

Coming into the town from the south, travellers cross a bridge on which, for a long time, there has been a chantry chapel. It is probable that a chapel was built on the bridge in 1362; the occasion was the progress of Edward III throughout the kingdom in commemoration of his having completed his fiftieth year. There has been some controversy among historians about whether it was in the reign of Edward III or Edward IV that the bridge was built. The weight of opinion and proof is in favour of the bridge being built in Edward III's reign but that it was re-endowed in the reign of Edward IV.

Its cresset light acted as a guide to the wayfarer and the navigator on the Calder. It was also visited by travellers who wished to give thanks in a chapel dedicated to the Virgin for their preservation from danger by 'flood and field', a quaint and archaic expression, perhaps meaning preservation from being killed on the field of battle. The chapel has undergone many changes – having been an old clothes shop, a warehouse, a shop for flax dressers, a news room, a cheesecake house and a tailor's shop.

Viewpoints on Huddersfield differed – a writer towards the end of the eighteenth century said that the place was 'Exceeding populous but the houses are meanly built and the streets irregular and ill paved'.[5] John Wesley said in 1757, 'A wilder people I never saw in England.'[6] In 1844 Friedrich Engels thought it 'the handsomest by far of all the factory towns of Yorkshire and Lancashire by reason of its charming situation and modern architecture'.[7]

Descriptions of places are nearly always subjective, and allowing for this, and for differences in date, it is possible that all these could have been true. Certainly by the time that Engels wrote there had been great improvements in Huddersfield. Joseph Kaye, a local man who was an engineer and a builder, gave the town two-storey houses of clean-cut stone, wide streets, the waterworks offices, St Paul's Church and the Royal Infirmary. There was an Improvement Act in 1820, and in 1821

the Huddersfield Gas Works Company came into being, eventually supplying gas to 650 street lamps which had been provided by the Improvement Commissioners. A plan of 1826 shows
the layout of the streets, but even though Huddersfield was
unmistakably a town, it was nothing approaching the size it is
today, being quite rural with tentercrofts for instance very near
the parish church and bordering Northgate and Union Street.

The lords of the manor of Huddersfield were the Ramsden
family, to whom the manor had been granted in the reign of
Elizabeth I, and they retained the land until they sold the manor
to Huddersfield Corporation in 1920. Within about a hundred
years of the original grant they had managed to get almost all of
the central area of Huddersfield and much of the east and south
parts of the County Borough, an area of land which was about
four thousand acres.

An amusing story, which may or may not be true but which
probably contains a germ of truth, is told about the Ramsden
monopoly. There was a small piece of land not in Ramsden
ownership, and the head of the family wanted to acquire it.
Accordingly he approached the owner, a true Yorkshireman,
but was consistently met with refusals: 'Nay, as long as this land
is mine, Huddersfield belongs to me and thee.' A final offer was
made which said that the land would be paved with sovereigns,
the number required being the purchase price. At last the owner
showed interest. 'Nah then,' he said. 'Ah'll sell if tha'll put 'em
on edge.' There was no sale.

Huddersfield was growing fast; in the 1820s and 1830s her
industry was increasingly important. There was considerable
feeling that the town should be fully responsible for its own
affairs, and by 1841 this feeling had come to a head, and a
petition signed by 2,505 inhabitants who represented a rateable
value of £23,021 was presented to the Privy Council asking for a
Charter of Incorporation. But there was also a considerable body
of opinion which did not wish to see change, and they presented
a counter-petition asking for things to be left as they were. 133
people signed this but they represented about £18,885 of rateable value. Unfortunately for the town, these petitions coin-
cided with a change of government at Westminster, and the new
Privy Council rejected the request for incorporation. An appli-

cation was made instead for increased local powers, and an
Improvement Act was passed in 1848; the Improvement Commissioners appointed under the terms of this Act did a worth-
while job. But Huddersfield, surrounded as it was by townships
– Deighton, Bradley, Fartown, Lindley, Lockwood, Moldgreen,
Newsome, Longwood and Almondbury, which each had their
own Boards of Health – found it difficult to co-ordinate schemes
for things like drainage and water supply. In 1867 the Improvement Commissioners suggested that a Charter of Incorporation
should be applied for to embrace Huddersfield and the surrounding townships.

Opinion had shifted but there were still some people opposed
to a charter, and Sir John Ramsden was anxious to safeguard his
position. The Charter was issued on 7 July 1868, and no reference was made to the Ramsden interests.

It was not until 1881 that Huddersfield acquired a new town
hall, which cost £57,000, and to celebrate the opening there was
a three-day festival at which Sir Charles Hallé said that the
Huddersfield Choral Society was the best choir he had ever
conducted. The town hall, which stands in Ramsden Street, is
neither so ornate nor so impressive as those of Halifax, Leeds
and Bradford, but is a modest building of pleasing proportions
and fits well with the more modern developments near it. It is
famous for its acoustics, and the town noted for its choral
society. Very near the town hall, in Princess Alexandra Walk, is
the library, and opposite that is a modern shopping precinct and
market hall.

The landscaped garden adjacent to this is an attractive and
much-needed oasis in the middle of a busy town. Huddersfield is
a good shopping centre with well-planned streets, and although
much of the building is new, among the modernity there are
several handsome buildings of a former age, the County Court
and Queen Square for instance, as well as several attractive
buildings in Byram Street. Ultra-modern, however, and in spite
of this quite attractive, are the sculptures on the outside of the
market hall which fronts onto the ring road, giving an extremely favourable impression to travellers through the town. Right
in the town centre, apparently at the heart of its affairs, which is
precisely where it should be, is the parish church, a large

nineteenth-century building surrounded by a garden with flower-beds and seats, a restful area much appreciated by shoppers and office workers at lunch time as well as by children who chase the pigeons.

But by far the most splendid architecture in Huddersfield, outdoing even the town hall, is the entrance to the railway station, 1847–50. Inside, the station is nondescript, but the magnificent classical façade is indeed handsome. The centre part, the main entrance, is flanked by two lower but symmetrical portions also in classical style. At one time the station was shared by two railway companies, and their coats of arms are still in evidence on the buildings at either side of the main entrance, the arms of the Lancashire and Yorkshire Railway Company at one side, those of the Huddersfield and Manchester Railway and Canal Company at the other. The splendid façade fills one side of a square, open at the bottom, while the other sides are occupied by the George Hotel and the offices of a building society.

One of the most notable citizens of Huddersfield – by adoption – was Richard Oastler, the factory king. He was born on 20 December 1789 in Leeds, where his father was a cloth merchant. The latter was a deeply religious man who shared the opinion of many workers in industry that the introduction of machinery meant misery and degradation to the poor, who would be even more oppressed by the rich. Accordingly he felt that he could no longer earn his living from the woollen industry and found himself a new job as head agent to Thomas Thornhill at Fixby, near Huddersfield.

At this time, Richard, aged eleven, was attending the Moravian School at Fulneck. At seventeen he was apprenticed to an architect at Wakefield, and it was while he was there that he did some electioneering for William Wilberforce – a Tory, while the Oastlers were Whigs. But Richard held the view that the abolition of slavery, for which Wilberforce stood, was a cause which was important enough to transcend party politics. Bad eyesight compelled him, after four years, to abandon his architectural training, and he went into business in Leeds as a drysalter, oilman, general dealer and chapman, and for the first time came into contact with poor people whose cause he championed and whose condition made a lasting impression on him.

In 1816, when he was twenty-seven, he married Mary Tatham, who came from Nottingham, and their early years of married life were very happy. However, in 1819 treble tragedy struck: two children born in the first and last months of the year died within a few days of birth, and Oastler went bankrupt. He managed to pay off his creditors, and the following year, when his father died, he succeeded him at Fixby. It was Fixby which made him a Tory and a member of the Established Church.

While he was at Fixby he met John Wood, a factory-owner in Bradford who told him that the working conditions of children in the textile factories were just as bad as those of the slaves in the West Indies. Oastler was appalled. Writing to the *Leeds Mercury* under the heading 'Yorkshire Slavery', he delivered a strong attack on those who allowed these conditions in the mills to continue, and by doing so he opened the floodgates of a furious controversy.

By the early 1830s groups of workers were agitating not only for shorter hours for children but also for better conditions for themselves. Short-time committees were formed and in June 1831 a deputation from these came to see Oastler at Fixby Hall, inviting him to be their leader. He agreed – the agreement being known as 'the Fixby Hall compact'. Fixby Hall was the headquarters of the movement, which was joined by textile workers from other counties. In March 1832 the Ten Hours Bill came up for its second reading and 'King Richard', 'The Factory King', now organized a demonstration in York, every town in the county to send a contingent. This meant, of course, walking, and for many this was a journey of 120 miles there and back. Rest stations were arranged along the route which would supply beer, bread and cheese, and each contingent brought its own band and home-made banners. From Bradford, Huddersfield and Halifax, three columns of men converged on Leeds, where the bells of the parish church rang out a welcome.

Unfortunately there was a terrible thunderstorm as the first men marched out of Leeds just before midnight, and the sodden and footsore men arrived at the Knavesmire to find that the bread and cheese ordered for them had not turned up. Richard Oastler, who had gone on ahead, hearing of their condition, borrowed a horse and rode to the Knavesmire to address them. The sight of him, as footsore and weary as they were, put new heart into the men. Some food had been acquired, which was distributed, and the meeting, attended by 25,000 people including MPs, ministers of religion and doctors as well as mill-workers, took place. When Oastler arrived home at Fixby and pulled off his socks, the skin of his feet came off with them. But the Bill failed to get through Parliament.

Mr Thornhill, the owner of Fixby Hall and Richard Oastler's employer, was becoming increasingly uneasy about the inflammatory speeches made by Oastler and, conscious of the fact that his home was the hotbed of revolutionary fervour, he dismissed his agent. Oastler's friends organized support and raised a subscription to provide him with an annuity. Fifteen thousand flag-waving, banner-carrying, cheering supporters organized his departure from Fixby.

In the meantime he was the victim of a mean trick. He had, during the time he had worked at Fixby and with the full consent of his employer, borrowed money from the estate to finance his campaign, money which he was paying back from his salary. At the time he was dismissed he had not finished paying it back, so his late employer accused him of embezzlement – later changing his charge to one of debt. Oastler never denied the charge of debt and was willing to repay the sum by instalments, but Thornhill refused, demanding the full sum, and as Oastler was unable to pay this, he had to go to the Debtors' Prison. Meanwhile his friends agitated on his behalf and raised a fund by which to pay his debt. By 1844, when they had raised £2,000, it was clear that his health was deteriorating, so his friends borrowed the remaining £600 and he walked out a free man.

The Ten Hour Bill was again rejected in 1846 but the following year John Fielden carried it through, and it was made law in June 1847.

An observation of a nineteenth-century satirist who penned his witticisms about Bradford is the following: 'After dark, on winter nights, when all the factories and warehouses are lit up, the town looks exceedingly picturesque, – prettier perhaps than if the streets had been more regularly built.'[8] This is very interesting in the light of a passage which was written by the late Wilfred Pickles:

Although only twelve, I had vivid memories of the unique Northern beauty of the mills in winter. No dirt or smoke, only light. I wondered, every time I saw thé spectacle, just how many people were busy behind those windows, which threw out gleams that made the wet pavements glisten, and the streets friendly. On cold rainy nights, the mills looked anything but 'dark and Satanic'. There was a warmth and a proud challenge in the solid mass of light which suggested an activity that went on without supervision and in all weathers. It was something I never took for granted. I used to stand and feel an admiration for the people who kept the mills going, and I longed to be in there with them.[9]

He was, of course, quite right; there is something unique, enchanting and enticing about the rows and rows of lit windows in the factories, something which has almost passed out of life now. And what better place in which to see this than Halifax.

Halifax is built in a hollow so that most roads out of the town have to climb. Coming into the town from either of the Bradford routes, one gets a bird's eye view of the place, particularly from the Shibden route; as one comes out of the Godley cutting, the entire town lies spread out in a vast panorama. Crossley's works at Dean Clough must have been an impressive sight as the mills, seven in all, seem to fill the clough, or narrow valley. Unfortunately, due to the recent recession, they have closed, a sense of shock sweeping over the town when the news broke. As someone said, 'Crossley's *is* Halifax.'

John Crossley, the founder of the firm, was a member of a Yorkshire family which had been settled in the area for a long time. He learned the business of carpet-weaving with an uncle, afterwards becoming manager of a small carpet-manufacturing firm which was carried on in Lower George Yard, Halifax; for some time he and his wife lived in a small house in the Lower George Yard. He continued as manager until Mr Job Lees, the owner of the firm, died, whereupon he and a couple of friends united their resources, bought the plant and carried on the business in partnership for some time. However, there were differences between them, and Mr Crossley then entered into partnership with his brother Thomas and another gentleman. They took a small mill, Dean Clough, on lease, and there carried on the business chiefly in worsted spinning. At the same time as working on his own account, Crossley continued to spin and dye the yarns and manage the looms of the firm he had left. After some time a crisis arose: the old firm began to send its wool elsewhere to be dyed and spun, and Crossley's firm encountered severe financial difficulties. Mrs Crossley, who came from farming stock, proved to be a tower of strength, and with thrift and hard work the firm pulled through.

Mrs Crossley herself worked in the firm and she wrote: 'In addition to carpet making we carried on the manufacture of shalloons and plainbacks, the whole of which I managed myself, so far as putting out the warps and weft and taking from the weavers.'[10] At this time carpets were not used universally; they tended to be a luxury for the rich so that the quality needed to be good.

The association of John Crossley and his two partners lasted for twenty years, and at the end of that time they dissolved the partnership quite amicably and Crossley continued the business in his own name, his sons, John, Joseph and Francis, coming into the business when they were old enough, the firm eventually being known as John Crossley & Sons.

After the death of John Crossley in 1837, the firm was carried on by his three sons and went from success to success, finances proving so sound that the property at Dean Clough was bought from Messrs Waterhouse, from whom it had been leased. Great extensions were made and also improvements in the machinery used. At the time that the three brothers took charge of the firm, machines were replacing hand looms, but in the carpet-weaving business there were certain difficulties, and no machine existed which was adequate to overcome them. However, little by little the energetic action of the Crossleys, helped by the inventive skill they had the good sense to employ, succeeded in bringing about the desired result. They became the proprietors of a series of patent rights and for some time enjoyed a monopoly of the trade.

At the time Mrs Crossley was working at the Dean Clough Mill she made a vow that, 'If the Lord does bless us at this place, the poor shall taste of it.' The Lord did, and the poor did.

The Crossleys used their wealth and talents for the benefit of the town. In 1852 Francis became the Liberal MP for Halifax, and he sat until 1859, when he was asked to contest the West Riding. He was returned and sat until 1867, after which he became MP for the Northern Division of the Riding; in 1863 a baronetcy was conferred on him. In 1855 he gave the people of Halifax the People's Park, which is out on the road to Lanca- shire, not far from the town centre.

The story behind this is interesting; while visiting the White Mountains in the USA, he was so entranced with the beauty of the scenery that he felt he would like to make a place of beauty for the enjoyment of all in his own town. Rejecting the Clare Hall site at the opposite end of the town, he chose the present site which is very near Belle Vue, where he lived (which until early 1983 was the central library). He called in Joseph Paxton, the designer of the Crystal Palace, who planned the park, which cost over £30,000, in addition to which he gave the Corporation £6,300 for its maintenance.

John Crossley junior, another of the brothers, was also a philanthropist, but he lacked the strong will and purpose of his brother Francis. He did sterling work in public life, serving on Halifax Town Council after the town had been incorporated as a borough in 1848; he also served on the School Board and as an MP. Joseph, the third brother, was essentially a businessman and did not figure in public life.

People's Park is still in existence as a beautiful monument to the Crossley family, but there are other tangible expressions of their munificence, including the Crossley and Porter Schools. These developed from the foundation by the firm of the Crossley Orphan Home and School which was built at a cost of £50,000 and endowed with approximately 3,000 a year. It was opened in 1864, designed to afford orphan children a liberal education with board and lodging, and could accommodate between two and three hundred children of both sexes. Each child was expected to pay from £5 to £10 a year as an acknowledgement, with the exception of forty who were maintained by the foun- dation. Children were admitted from six years of age and upwards, boys being kept until the age of fifteen and girls until seventeen.

In 1855 Francis Crossley built and endowed twenty-two alms-houses near Belle Vue, the endowment providing an allowance of 8s. 6d. a week to each male inmate and 6s. to each female.

Coming into Halifax from Queensbury, one passes Akroydon, the model village which was built by Colonel Edward Akroyd, a member of another prominent textile manufacturing family in Halifax. For much of the nineteenth century the Crossleys and the Akroyds were the main employers in the town. Like other mill-owners in the area – Sir Titus Salt and the Fielden brothers for example – the Akroyds were progressive employers. One of the methods adopted by Colonel Akroyd to improve the conditions of the poor was to promote thrift by establishing penny savings banks. The first of these, opened in 1852, was the Woodside Penny Savings Bank, which was subsequently removed to Haley Hill, occupying the building which was used as a Baptist chapel. This endeavour preceded the foundation of the Yorkshire Penny Bank in 1859. In 1855 the Haley Hill Working Men's College was founded by Colonel Akroyd in order to enable those whose education had been neglected in their youth to get an elementary education at evening classes and also to enable others to continue their day-time education.

In conjunction with a local building society, he formed a company to build model dwelling-houses for his workers. These, built in the domestic Gothic style, have a regular and pleasing appearance, the names of the streets reflecting his interests in cathedrals: Beverley, Ripon, York, Salisbury and Chester. Across the road a big mansion house, Bankfield, which is now a museum, was Colonel Akroyd's residence, while further down still is the church of All Saints, Haley Hill, which was his greatest gift to Halifax. It is a slender and graceful structure built in the thirteenth-century Decorated style.

On the western outskirts of the town lies Savile Park, a great stretch of open land which in 1866 was conceded to the town by Captain Savile, who gave up his manorial rights for a nominal sum of £100. On the edge of this is the Albert Promenade, also known locally as the Rocks Promenade, from which there is a superb view of the lower Calder Valley and the Ryburn Valley. Another of Halifax's fine parks is Manor Heath, which was bought by the Corporation in 1929 for £18,500.

Near Savile Park at the western end of the town is a lofty and slender tower, Wainhouse Tower, built by a man named John Edward Wainhouse. He was born in 1817 and about the middle of the century or just after inherited from an uncle some dyeworks along with several other properties. In common with other industrial towns at that time Halifax was affected by thick smoky fog caused by the factories – of which the dyeworks was one – belching forth smoke. When one of John Wainhouse's wealthy neighbours, Sir Henry Edwards, complained about the smoke nuisance of the dyeworks, he had the idea of building a tall chimney high on the hillside above the dyeworks with an underground flue or tunnel linking chimney and dyeworks, which was quite a common practice at this time. It is thought that he asked an architect to design and build such a chimney and also, and these are the interesting facts, to build a staircase inside it and to make the edifice aesthetically pleasing.

Wainhouse may have been planning mischief against his neighbour Sir Henry Edwards, who boasted that from no house on the hills round his estate at Pye Nest could a view be obtained of his private grounds – otherwise why the staircase? At any rate, on hearing of this boast, Wainhouse vowed that he would alter all that and asked the architect to construct an observatory at the top of the mill chimney. At this point Isaac Booth, who was also the architect for Sir Henry Edwards, declared that he could no longer work for both of them and chose to continue his work for Sir Henry. Wainhouse then appointed Richard Swarbrick Dugdale, who redesigned the upper section of the tower. The building was started in 1871 and completed in 1875, using stone which was quarried and dressed locally and hauled up the inside of the chimney in order to be put in place. It is estimated that more than 9,000 tons of material were used and that the cost was about £15,000. The height of the tower is 253 feet, and there are 400 steps, making it clear that it was really never intended to have been used as a chimney. In 1883 Wainhouse died. Calderdale Metropolitan Council eventually came into possession of the tower; it is open to the public from time to time, usually on Bank Holidays, and from it there is a splendid view.

After Halifax received its Charter of Incorporation, there was pressure for a new town hall to be built, an idea which was opposed by influential citizens who said it would be too costly. Power to build one was embodied in the Improvement Act of 1853 although it was ten years before it became a reality. In the meantime the newly established Town Council met in the old assembly rooms behind the old Talbot Hotel. As local government responsibility grew and departments increased, it became imperative that there should be a town hall, and discussion came to a head in May 1858 when the Council voted to build a hall in Crossley Street. A public meeting attended by a thousand people voted to support this. In April 1861 there was a ceremonial stone-laying, and in August 1863 the town hall was opened by HRH the Prince of Wales. In addition to people from Halifax, visitors came from all over the county; it was estimated that anywhere up to a hundred thousand people watched either the ceremony itself or part of the procession. On no other occasion have the street decorations in Halifax been so elaborate. Large platforms and galleries were built at suitable places round the town to enable people to see. The West Yorkshire towns seem to have had no luck with their opening ceremonies – it rained at this one, as it had done at Leeds and was later to do at Bradford. In the Piece Hall, fifteen thousand Sunday School children and a large number of others were assembled to sing hymns and the 'Hallelujah Chorus' to celebrate the occasion.

The multiplicity of local government functions brought about, in the 1970s, a replay of the conditions which made it necessary to build the town hall in the first place. Departments were scattered, libraries and archives being at Belle Vue, while education was housed in premises vacated by the Halifax Building Society. New premises were built and occupied in 1982, thus centralizing several scattered departments.

Defoe described at great length the cloth market in Leeds which had grown too big for its location near the bridge and was held in the main street, which was then Briggate, the street laid out by Maurice Paynel in 1207 when he obtained a charter to create a new town. On each side of this street were approximately thirty burgage plots, the sites on which houses and workshops were built. In Defoe's day it would have been a handsome street, still quite rural, bordered by large houses with gardens, orchards and stables. At the bottom of this street ran Boar Lane, and higher up was Kirkgate, leading to St Peter's Church, while parallel to Briggate was Vicar Lane, and crossing the top of both the Headrow, just beyond which was another church, St John's. Further up Briggate than its junction with Kirkgate was the town hall, the shambles, where meat was sold, and the market cross.

Defoe described Leeds as a 'large, wealthy and populous town', and in fact its population had increased so much that it had become impossible for the two existing churches, St Peter's and St John's, to accommodate all the worshippers. Plans were therefore drawn up to build a new church, which was opened in 1727; this was Holy Trinity, Boar Lane. Holy Trinity Church was built by public subscription, people contributing both large and small amounts of money; Lady Elizabeth Hastings gave £1,000 and, surprisingly, there was a contribution from the Corporation of Newcastle-upon-Tyne. The church, which stands almost as close as it is possible to be to the newest shopping complex in Leeds, the Bond Street Centre, is built in the Later English Renaissance style of architecture from durable moor stone (similar to that quarried at Bramley Fall), some it quarried at Meanwood. The tower, which is impressive and stands out on the skyline (it has been said that the architect used some of Wren's plans in his work), rises in three stages from the roof, and the whole is capped by a sort of cupola surmounted by a cross. The tower contains two bells, the older of which, dating from 1728, is the oldest church bell in Leeds. Although the area has been almost denuded of parishioners – attempts have been made to close the church completely – its work continues. Midday communion services draw in people who work in the city centre; there is a counselling service for the lonely, and the forecourt is used for exhibitions to highlight social problems and draw attention to the need for programmes of famine relief, help the aged and so on.

About a century later Leeds was described as being 'chiefly composed of one large street with others branching from it'.[11] The writer also observed that, 'New buildings are formed with an attention to both elegance and convenience, the modern parts being uniform and genteel.'[12] Another nineteenth-

A very fine doorway in the Little Germany district in Bradford

This fine building in Little Germany, Bradford, was once a warehouse, a section of it is now used by the Department of Health and Social Security

The Tyrls and the Law Courts, Bradford

Halifax Town Hall with its impressive clock tower. An imposing
building which conveys a feeling of solid assurance

A pleasant modern shopping centre in Huddersfield

Modern shop fronts in one of Huddersfield's pedestrian precincts

The magnificent façade of Huddersfield Railway Station. At one time the station was shared by the Lancashire and Yorkshire Railway and the Huddersfield and Manchester Railway

The entrance to Leeds Art Gallery and the Henry Moore Sculpture Centre

Leeds Civic Centre—'Our house' as the Lord Mayor called it—which celebrated its Golden Jubilee in 1983

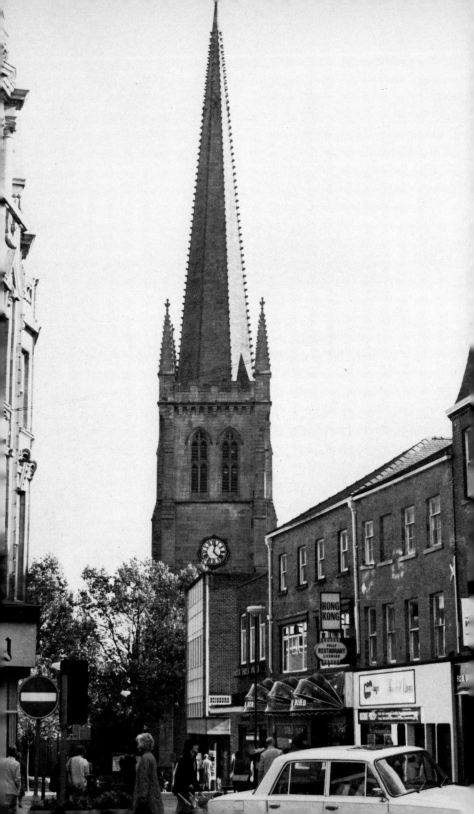

Above: Wood Street, Wakefield, showing County Hall and Wakefield Town Hall

Left: Wakefield Cathedral stands right in the heart of the city

Shoppers and office workers enjoy the autumn sun at the south side
of Wakefield Cathedral

century visitor spoke of it as one of the most commercial and opulent towns in Yorkshire and was impressed by the elegance and handsomeness of the buildings and the fine streets in parts of the town, being particularly impressed by the gracious square and by the churches, five by now, St Paul's, St James, St Peter's, St John's and Holy Trinity. But he spoke of the south of the city as disagreeable.

Many visitors to Leeds seemed interested in the manufacturing industry in the mills, and above all in the markets and the cloth halls. One, however, of an inquiring and original mind, made comments of a different nature about Leeds. He was amazed, writing in the 1820s, that Leeds, with 120,000 inhabitants, had no member of Parliament whereas 'many a wretched ruined village sends 2 members.' He reached Leeds in the twilight and described what he saw: 'A transparent cloud of smoke was diffused over the whole space which it occupies . . . a hundred red fires shot upwards into the sky and as many towering chimneys poured forth columns of black smoke. The huge manufactories, five storeys high in which every window was illuminated had a grand and striking effect.'[13] His remarks on food are interesting, not especially for the light they shed on the history of Leeds or necessarily on Yorkshire hospitality but on the custom of the age. He appeared to be travelling and, on this occasion, dining alone. On his table for supper/dinner, was 'a cold ham, an awful roast beef [why awful we are not told, but as he was a German he probably meant it in its now archaic sense of full of awe], a leg of mutton, a piece of roast veal, a hare pie, a partridge, three sorts of pickle, cauliflowers cooked in water, potatoes, butter and cheese. This would have been meat enough to feed a whole party of German burghers.'[14]

The geography of the city centre streets is much as it was in the days of Defoe and the later travellers, although activity near the bridge has changed. Below Leeds Bridge the river flows, silent, black and murky, because other forms of transport have superseded river boats. The canal basin is surrounded by warehouses, gaunt and forbidding, reminders of an age of commercial bustle and busy wharves; it is only when there is an inland waterways rally that the canal basin hums with life and the area is crowded with gaily coloured holiday craft.

Shopping centres of large towns have ceased to have a great interest for the traveller. As privately owned shops and large stores have been superseded by nationally known multiple stores, one knows beforehand much of what one will find in the principal streets of the main towns. There is the green of one, the red of another and the blue of another, and Leeds is no exception.

Through the blocks of shops which fill the city centre are arcades which date from late Victorian times when the premises were built. These make the Leeds city centre, if not unique, certainly different, and the development of the arcades is interesting. The owners of the houses in Briggate, with their gardens behind, subdivided their plots of land, and by the early nineteenth century it was usual for them to be built on so that there were houses and cottages down the yard. As trade and commerce increased and merchants and clothiers arrived in Briggate to buy and sell cloth, it was sensible that occupiers of some of these houses should provide them with refreshment as they waited for the market bell to announce the beginning of trading. Many of the yards therefore contained an inn; some still do.

One of the innkeepers was Charles Thornton who kept the 'Old White Swan' in Swan Street, off Briggate. He was also the proprietor of the Varieties Music Hall, now the City Varieties, and in 1875 he received permission to rebuild the Old Talbot Inn in Briggate and to erect a new arcade of shops on the site of the inn yard. Thornton's Arcade has three storeys and is celebrated not because it was the first of the arcades but because it has an entertaining clock. There are four life-like characters taken from Sir Walter Scott's *Ivanhoe*: Friar Tuck and Richard Cœur de Lion strike the hours alternately, while Robin Hood and Garth the Swineherd strike the quarters.

The second arcade was built in the year of Queen Victoria's Golden Jubilee on the site of the 'Rose and Crown' yard and is known as Queen's Arcade; this has a second storey of shops. In 1898 two new arcades were built, the Victoria Arcade, since demolished to accommodate extensions by a large store, and the Grand Arcade, which, like Thornton's Arcade, has an entertaining clock. On either side of the clock stand two knights in armour, while on the hour five figures emerge on a revolving stage, a guardsman, a Scotsman, an Irishman, a Canadian and an Indian. The last to be built was County Arcade on the site of 'White Horse' yard.

In the middle of all this bustle and commerce, there are oases of peace and serenity, such as the pedestrian precincts with generous seating provision and the fairly recently created Dortmund Square which is on the Headrow, Dortmund being the twin town of Leeds; the square was officially opened in 1980 by the Mayor of Dortmund, who unveiled a statue of a German miner.

There are also spiritual oases of peace: Holy Trinity, on Boar Lane, is one; St John's Church in Briggate, lying just behind Lewis's, is another. This church, consecrated by the Archbishop of York on 21 September 1634, was founded and endowed by John Harrison, a citizen of Leeds who was, at the time of the consecration of the church, an alderman of the corporation for a second time. He endowed it with £80 per annum and also left £10 yearly to keep it in repair. Externally the building gives the impression of a late fifteenth-century church rather than an early seventeenth-century foundation. Dr Whitaker, the eminent antiquary, disliked the interior of the church, which he thought was full of gloom, but while it is true that the woodwork is rather dark and heavy, it has a mellow, warm aspect and some of the carving is of great beauty. In addition to founding the church, Harrison also founded the nearby almshouses, now demolished, and a free grammar school which developed into Leeds Grammar School, and he also provided the market cross.

Cheek by jowl with the Bond Street shopping centre, at the opposite end from Holy Trinity Church, is the gracious building of Mill Hill Chapel, the Unitarian chapel at which Joseph Priestley, the discoverer of oxygen, was minister from 1767 for a period of six years. It was while he was in Leeds that he experimented, discovering the nature of different gases, and in 1772 he published a paper announcing the discovery of marine acid gas (hydrochloric acid) and nitrous air (nitrous oxide). He also discovered a method of impregnating water with fixed air (carbon dioxide), producing what we know as soda water, which he recommended as a drink for sailors to prevent scurvy. As a theologian, it was he who invented the phrase, 'the greatest happiness of the greatest number', usually associated with Jeremy Bentham, who in fact did use it. Well ahead of his time, Priestley advocated religious toleration.

Moving away from the city centre shopping area, one finds the tangible manifestation of the nineteenth-century urban expansion of Leeds, the education offices, the museum, the art gallery and public library and the town hall. The commercial and industrial development of Leeds gathered momentum during the nineteenth century, and by 1850 some of the prominent citizens wanted a new town hall. In 1852 a competition was announced for its design, and Sir Charles Barry, who designed the Houses of Parliament, was asked to judge. Cuthbert Brodrick, an architect from Hull, was the winner and was awarded the prize of £200 for his superb Renaissance-style building.

Queen Victoria, who performed the opening ceremony on 7 September 1858, is reported to have come to Leeds by train and stayed overnight at the home of the Lord Mayor, Peter Fairburn. Unfortunately, the day of the opening was damp and cloudy with drizzling rain, but the poor weather in no way deterred the citizens of Leeds, who came out in their thousands to see their Queen; it was estimated that between 150,000 and 200,000 people turned up. On Woodhouse Moor, a large tract of open land not far from the city centre, a great crowd of people was assembled: 32,000 children from the various Sunday Schools in Leeds as well as more than 60,000 adults. It was of course unlikely in an age as disciplined as the Victorian that there would be any untoward or rowdy behaviour but it is amusing to read that there were signalmen appointed, not to control the crowd but to direct their reactions. The signalmen carried boards on which were printed instructions to the crowds such as 'Prepare to cheer', 'Sing', 'Silence' and 'Dismiss'.

The main hall of the town hall was originally referred to as 'the Great Hall' but after the official opening it was dedicated to the Queen and called 'the Victoria Hall'. Recently cleaned, redecorated and restored, it is a splendid sight. In design and colouring the restorers have remained faithful to the original; the ceiling is divided into five bays, each of which is richly ornamented, the decorative panels being painted in midnight blue and sky blue. Likewise the walls are divided by Corinthian pillars into five bays which contain panels in corn yellow bounded by grey green, while the cornice caps and entablatures to the columns are decorated in ivory which is richly gilded. Over the semicircular window at the back of the hall, where originally there was a coat of arms of the city and the gilds of local crafts, some alteration has been made; the original coats of arms have been replaced by those of the seven constituent authorities making up the new Leeds Metropolitan Council. These are the arms of Rothwell, Wetherby, Pudsey, Leeds, Otley, Morley and Aireborough. In order to carry out this restoration work 225 gallons of paint were applied and the gilding used 800 books of 23-carat gold leaf (gold leaf is still produced, as it has been for centuries, by beating the soft gold with leather hammers until it is wafer thin).

Brodrick was also responsible for the design of the Corn Exchange, an impressive circular building at the other end of the city from the town hall, which is now used by several small firms and the main part hired out for shows and exhibitions.

The town hall was not used to accommodate the administrative offices of the local government departments; they were situated in the municipal buildings – currently occupied by the central library, museum and art gallery. Leeds had received its Charter of Incorporation in 1626, but the charter disappeared in the Civil War so that a new one was issued in 1661. The 1626 charter vested the government of the borough in an alderman, nine burgesses and twenty assistants under the corporate style of 'The Alderman and Burgesses of the Borough of Leeds in the County of York' which has been modified and improved through various Municipal Acts.

In the early centuries after the Charter of Incorporation there was little administrative business involved in looking after the town's affairs; the population was relatively small and neither expected nor received anything like the amenities expected by twentieth-century citizens as their right and due. But, by the late nineteenth century, with concepts of the function of local government widening and the population increasing, there was pressure on the space then available for the discharge of all the functions. As early as 1899 the town hall had proved inadequate for the administration of justice, and it was resolved that new law courts were imperative. New law courts were, in fact, opened in August 1982.

Other departments, however, had less time to wait. In 1928 the Finance and Parliamentary Committee appointed a sub-committee to consider and report on accommodation in the town hall and municipal buildings, and the report stated that there was no room for any expansion in either place. Early in 1930 therefore a scheme for the provision of a new civic building was submitted, and as there was high unemployment at this time, the scheme was accelerated with a view to providing work for some of the unemployed. A grant was made towards the scheme by the Unemployed Grants Committee subject to the proviso that the work was actively begun by 1 October 1930 and that the building was completed within 2½ years of its commencement.

The civic hall is a fine building standing behind the former municipal buildings; it has an impressive classical front with twin towers, and its complex slopes upwards from Great George Street having a garden of rest – used and appreciated by office workers who picnic there on fine summer lunch-times. The hall is faced with Portland stone and roofed with grey-green West-morland slate. The total area of the site is about three acres. The civic hall was opened by King George V and Queen Mary on 23 August 1933. In the autumn of 1982 a fierce row broke out about a decision to name the gardens immediately in front of the civil hall after Nelson Mandela.

There has been much modern building in Leeds; the central shopping area has been enriched by the creation of several pedestrian precincts, and the Bond Street Centre has been built. Behind City Square, on the site of the old cloth hall and on adjoining land, there are new office blocks named Cloth Hall Court, while behind the civic hall there is the vast complex of the polytechnic buildings. A sculpture centre has been added to the front of the present art gallery in honour of Henry Moore, while at the other side of the town hall new law courts have been opened.

From many directions the tall buildings, high-rise office blocks and flats form the skyline, but from almost every approach the Leeds scene is dominated by the great tower of the university's Parkinson Building. It was in 1874 that the Yorkshire College of Science first opened its doors, its schools consisting of four departments, mathematics and experimental physics, chemistry, geology and mining, and textiles, to which within the next three years were added schools of classics, English, history and French. In 1887 it became a constituent college of the new Victoria University of Manchester; a department of agriculture was added and also a small hall of residence, while in 1894 a new building was opened to house the enlarged School of Medicine.

Meanwhile events had been moving fast on the other side of the Pennines, and in 1903 the colleges at Manchester and Liverpool obtained separate charters permitting them to become universities in their own right. Leeds was not long in obtaining its charter, which was granted in 1904. One body of opinion wished the new seat of learning to be designated 'the University of Yorkshire' but this was (fortunately) overruled, and it was called 'the University of Leeds'. The number of subjects taught expanded greatly, and over the years there was an increase in the number of students and also in the acreage occupied by the university. In the decades following the War, this increase has been maintained.

In 1937 Frank Parkinson, then chairman of Crompton Parkinson and Company, manufacturers of electrical goods, and himself an old student of the Yorkshire College, supplemented a previous gift of £50,000 for scholarships by giving a further £200,000 for the erection of the building which bears his name. While his aim was to provide more dignified chambers for the Council and Senate, he also wished that the central block should include an entrance and an entrance hall which would leave an indelible impression on the mind of the student that he would regard in after years with affection.

Leeds stands unrivalled among the industrial cities of Britain for its amount of parkland in proportion to the population. Within the area of the old City of Leeds (that is, the city before local government reorganization) there are 4,815 acres of parks and open spaces out of a total acreage of 40,619 acres, and in addition to this Leeds preserved a green belt which amounts to about 30 per cent of its area. Roundhay Park, reputedly the finest park in the whole country, was a hunting-ground of the de

Laci family and was later hunted by John of Gaunt. Its transition from a private estate to a public park is interesting.

In 1804 the estate passed to the Nicholson family; in 1811 the Mansion House was built, and it was about this time that the park as it is now was taking shape. The big lake, formerly a quarry, took ten years to build at a cost of £15,000, being completed in 1815, an almost unbroken expense of thirty-three acres and, in honour of the British victory, named Waterloo Lake.

In 1868 the owner of the estate, William Nicholson, died, and as the family were unable to agree on the division of the estate, it was put up for auction. Sir John Barron suggested that it should be bought for the public of Leeds and used as a park, but at that time the law did not permit the council to spend more than £40,000 on a project of this nature, so he made the bold and magnanimous suggestion that he, together with a group of friends, should put up money for the purchase of the estate and they could later be reimbursed by the council. This is in fact what happened, and after much public debate the estate was bought. A committee of the House of Lords finally decided in favour of the purchase in the summer of 1872 at a cost of £139,000.

But it was not a popular decision; people regarded it as a white elephant, a waste of ratepayers' money, and wondered, in view of the fact that it was so far removed from any centre of population, just who was supposed to get any benefit from it. However, the building of a tramway there meant that it became easily accessible to all, and the controversy died down.

Roundhay Park is superb, so vast that it 'has everything'. There are two lakes, large areas of woodland through which one can walk, and open spaces on which public events are held from time to time. There are bowling-greens, a rose garden and, one of the most interesting features, the canal gardens, which were at one time the kitchen gardens of the estate. Here there are ducks on the canal, a fountain, flower-beds, a conservatory with colourful and exotic plants, tropical fish and a bird-house.

Different in character is Golden Acre Park, which had been developed as a botanical garden in which many plants, shrubs and trees have been established, especially those which are hardy in the north of England. The intention is to preserve there the existing flora and additional British plants which are not indigenous to the district.

And so to Bradford, or, to use the local idiom, Bratford. One of the difficulties to the natives of neither county is to distinguish between a Yorkshire and a Lancashire accent, and no greater insult can be handed out than to plump for the wrong one. To inhabitants of either county it is easier to spot the differences, and a Lancastrian has pointed out that a sure way of knowing Yorkshiremen is by the way they pronounce the name of the wool capital 'Bratford' – almost invariably they do.

Local government reorganization has done nothing to mitigate the rivalry between Bradford and Leeds. (Both places have a township, Allerton, which is 'Ollerton' in Bradford and 'Allerton', with an 'a' as in 'cat', in Leeds.) It was the establishment of the St George's Hall in Bradford which spurred the people of Leeds to press for a town hall, while in turn the fact that Leeds had a town hall encouraged the Bradfordians to follow suit. But as Leeds had one in a classical style, Bradford opted for Gothic.

A wag who, over a hundred years ago, wrote satirical sketches about West Riding life, had several amusing things, also very true, to say about his fictitious town of Woolborough. To one having a lifelong acquaintance with the area, it is unmistakably Bradford, and although what is said was written in the mid 1870s, much is recognizable as true of more recent times.

Bradford, he said, had grown from obscurity to a place of considerable importance in the industrial world in less than three-quarters of a century. But, he went on, 'Woolborough is treated much in the same way as a great overgrown boy, with whose growth the tailors are unable to keep pace. Year by year its old streets are found too small to admit of a proper display of its strength and vigour; consequently the said streets are constantly being let out, patched and renovated. The Corporation is perpetually rushing up to Parliament to obtain extended powers and coming back and slicing the town in all directions.'[15]

How true this seems, for, unlike Leeds, Bradford appears to have no plan; there is no logical method by which one can find one's way through the town centre; one either knows or one doesn't. A good rule is, 'Follow the fall of your foot (i.e. walk downhill) and you will end either in Forster Square or in Town Hall Square.' Of course, since this interesting prose description was written there have been many changes – the Corporation rushing to Parliament to effect yet more changes. The satirist goes on to say that the Corporation were intent on 'rooting out of existence every remnant of antiquity that can possibly be found.'[16] Certainly this has been the practice in recent years when, in order to build new roads, nineteenth-century buildings of great character have been removed. Traffic flow in the town centre may have been increased, although this is dubious, but the quality of the environment has not.

'In Woolborough, it is the rule that if you are not going up, you are going down. . . .'[17] Again how true. Bradford is what is known as hard work to shoppers.

Much of what he says applies solely to Bradford, as of course it is intended to do, but there are one or two passages which could just as well have been applied to any of the textile-manufacturing towns in West Yorkshire until well into the present century: 'The town is . . . more full of tall chimney-towers than an Eastern city is of minarets. These commercial beacons stud the landscape as closely as masts in a harbour and give the town quite a monumental aspect; and an air of funereal gloom is imparted to the place by the smoke-clouds which are emitted from these chimneys, and which hang sullenly over the factory tops. . . .'[18]

The fame of the town rests on wool – weren't the citizens supposed to have festooned the tower of the parish church with woolsacks in order to protect it from the worst ravages of war during the sieges of Bradford? Just as the Leeds skyline is dominated by the great white tower of the Parkinson Building of the University of Leeds, that of Bradford is dominated by Lister's mill chimney.

One of the features of the town's connection with wool was the septennial celebration of the festival of Bishop Blaize, the patron saint of wool-combers. His credentials as a candidate for sainthood seem to be worthy enough, but his connection with wool-combing seems to be so slender as scarcely to exist. He was Bishop of Sebaste in Armenia and, from his lifestyle, appears to have been a very sincere recluse. He lived in a cave in which he was visited daily by wild beasts who came to be cured by him. If, when they arrived, he was at prayer, they did not interrupt him but waited until he had finished and never departed without his benediction. He was martyred in 316. The last celebration of his festival in Bradford was in 1825.

The day was fine and favourable to this great outdoor event, and from an early hour the roads into Bradford were thronged with people pouring in from the small towns and villages outside. When one considers the public transport, or more accurately the lack of it, at this period, one cannot help but admire the stamina of our forebears who turned up to witness the processions of this nature. On the other hand spectacles and entertainments on this scale were few and far between, which gave an added incentive to attend while the going was good.

The procession was a splendid spectacle:

> The apprentices and masters' sons . . . formed the most showy part of the procession; their caps being richly ornamented with ostrich feathers, flowers, and knots of various coloured yarn; and their stuff garments formed of the gayest colours. Some of these dresses were very costly, from the profusion of their decorations.
>
> The shepherd, shepherdess, and swains were attired in bright green. The woolsorters, from their number, and the height of their plumes of feathers, which were mostly of different colours, formed in the shape of a fleur-de-lis, had a dashing appearance. The comb-makers carried before them the instruments here so much cele-brated, raised on standards, together with golden fleeces, rams' heads with gilded horns and other emblems. The wool-combers were neatly dressed, and looked mighty wise in their odd-fashioned and full flowing wigs of combed wool.[19]

The order of procession was as follows:

Herald, bearing a flag.

Twenty-four Woolstaplers on horseback, each horse caparisoned with a fleece.

Thirty-eight Worsted-Spinners and Manufacturers on horseback, in white stuff waistcoats, with each a sliver of wool over his shoulder and a white stuff sash: the horses' necks covered with nets made of thick yarn.

Six Merchants on horseback, with coloured sashes.

Three Guards.   Masters' Colours.   Three Guards.

Fifty-six Apprentices and Masters' Sons on horseback, with
ornamented caps, scarlet coloured coats, white stuff waistcoats, and
blue pantaloons.

Bradford and Keighley Bands.

Macebearer, on foot.

Six Guards.   KING.   QUEEN.   Six Guards.

Guards.   JASON.   PRINCESS MEDEA.   Guards.

Bishop's Chaplain.

BISHOP BLAIZE.

Shepherd and Shepherdess.

Shepherd-Swains.

One hundred and sixty Woolsorters on horseback, with ornamented
caps and various coloured slivers.

Thirty Comb-makers.

Charcoal Burners.

Combers' Colours.

Band.

Four hundred and seventy Wool-combers, with wool wigs, &c.

Band.

Forty Dyers, with red cockades, blue aprons, and crossed slivers of
red and blue.[20]

But there are more lasting monuments to Bradford's association with wool, one of which is in the town centre – the Wool
Exchange, a handsome building in Venetian Gothic style, the
floor of whose main hall was crowded on 'change days' with
merchants bidding for wool. From the middle of the nineteenth
century handsome warehouses were built in Bradford, the pro-
totype for architectural style being the Italian merchant palace.
They had marked horizontal lines which were richly moulded,

each storey divided from the next by carving, and the whole finished by a classical cornice. The Gothic style, although not unpleasing aesthetically, was not particularly practical; as Bradford's streets were not wide and the atmosphere was smoky and dark, the users of the Wool Exchange found that it was necessary to keep the gas lighting on for many hours in the day. During the nineteenth century more and more Germans began to settle in Bradford, and they built many fine warehouses, most of them in the Leeds road area just wide of the town centre – there are so many of them that the area is known as 'Little Germany'. They are, most of them, very tall buildings, having four or five storeys with wide windows and carved projecting sills between each storey, and the narrow streets accentuate their lofty appearance. Examined in detail, some of the door-ways show fine carving, sufficient to give interest and dignity and to add beauty to the buildings, but not enough to make them florid. Currently there is a scheme to spend money to convert some of these warehouses, now standing empty, to make them suitable for use as premises for small businesses.

As in other large towns, Bradford's population was expanding in the nineteenth century. In 1847 Bradford Corporation came into being, its administrative headquarters in the fire-station house in Swain Street. The increasing complexity of local government meant that it soon outgrew its home but it was not until the 1860s that it was definitely decided to build a new town hall; several sites were considered and in 1869 the present one was selected. Prizes were offered for the best design, the contract being awarded to the firm of Lockwood & Mawson, who submitted two designs, one classical, the other Gothic. The foundation stone was laid on 10 August 1870, and on 9 September 1873 the town hall was opened, the day of the opening being declared a public holiday and the celebrations lasting three days. Mr Gladstone was invited to perform the opening ceremony but was unable to oblige, so the Earl of Derby was asked, and as he also was not able to help, in the end the honour fell to the Mayor.

Before the opening ceremony there was a grand procession of trades which consisted of twelve thousand people representing forty-five different trades and no fewer than seventeen bands – it was so long that it took two hours to pass a given point. People

came from far and wide and the roads were thronged with
carriages and carts; those without means of transport came on
foot, while business on the railways boomed and trains dis-
gorged thousands of passengers. Platforms and balconies were
put up, and houses and business premises decorated with flags,
banners and streamers in honour of the great event. Unfortunately the occasion was marred by rain but, as the local paper
said, 'Yorkshiremen have a sturdy contempt for the milksops
who shrink from the mischance of a wet jacket.'

Although Bradford was developing as a commercial and industrial centre and mills and houses were growing apace, there
was a lack of a hall for public meetings. Older-established towns
such as Leeds and Wakefield had their assembly rooms. There
was in Bradford the exchange buildings and the mechanics'
institute which were used for meetings and concerts, but even
these were not enough. In 1849 a company was formed with the
idea of a building a suitable music hall, and £16,000 was
subscribed in £10 shares. A site was chosen at the junction of
Hall Ings and Bridge Street, and St George's Hall, a very fine
building, was erected.

Bradford's claim to fame has been as the wool capital of the
world but the town was also a leader in the educational field. It
was an MP for Bradford, W. E. Forster, who was largely responsible for steering the Education Act of 1870 through Parliament, and his statue stands in Forster Square. He was not a
Yorkshireman by birth, being born in Dorset, the only child of a
Quaker minister, but Yorkshire became his adopted county. He
came to Bradford in 1841, and in 1842 joined William Fison in
partnership in a textile business, Waterloo Mill, their original
factory, being in the centre of Bradford. In 1850 they transferred
their business to Burley in Wharfedale, and were model employers who provided many facilities for their workers. In 1850
Forster married Jane Arnold, the daughter of the late Dr
Thomas Arnold of Rugby. Thus he was the son-in-law of the
headmaster who did an enormous amount to reform and modernize the English public school system, and the brother-in-law
of an inspector of schools, Matthew Arnold, who was also a poet.
It is fitting therefore that it should be an educational reform for
which he is best remembered. His marriage outside the faith of

the Quakers constituted a mixed marriage, and he consequently was no longer one of them; he then became a member of the Anglican Church. Soon after his marriage he set up house in Burley in Wharfedale. His parliamentary career may be said to have begun in 1859 when he unsuccessfully contested the Leeds seat, but after the retirement of Mr (later Sir) Titus Salt, he was returned unopposed for Bradford in 1861. From this time he represented the town until his death in 1886. He was buried at Burley in Wharfedale.

Bradford pioneered the way in the matter of nursery school education and also in the establishment of school medical services, much of this pioneering being done by Margaret McMillan. She was born in the USA in 1860, the child of Scottish parents, but her father died when she was young and her mother returned to Scotland with the two girls. Margaret and her sister Rachel received a middle-class upbringing, and Margaret was sent to Frankfurt-am-Main to study music. When the course was finished, she returned to Scotland to work as a governess but was converted to Socialism and moved to London, presumably to get more into the heart of politics. In London she led a mixed sort of life: she studied drama and worked as a companion, at the same time preaching Socialism and, by taking part in the dock strike of 1889, practising what she preached. Invited to go to Bradford to work for the newly formed Independent Labour Party, she arrived there in November 1893.

The following year she was elected to the School Board, becoming perhaps its most famous member. She claimed that it was her duty and privilege to fight the battle of the slum child and always voted in the interests of the child rather than those of the party; she pressed for more hygienic school buildings, lectures on child health, kindergarten methods for infant teaching, and better facilities for handicapped children. Many of her ideas bore fruit in Bradford; for example, during the First World War, when children suffered from lack of sleep, her recommendation that beds should be provided for the youngest children was implemented in 1915 at Whetley Lane Infants' School.

She wrote and spoke, when elected to the School Board, about the appalling conditions of children in schools and advocated medical inspections, nursery schools, school feeding and open-air schools. As a result of this, Dr Kerr undertook, probably in 1899, the first school medical inspection anywhere in the country, at Usher Street School.

In 1902 School Boards were abolished and Bradford Education Committee came into being; one of its early acts was to apply to the Board of Education to get permission to provide meals for poor children from public funds. By 1907 the school meals system had spread, and a central cooking depot was opened – the first in the country. Bradford started the first nursery school in the provinces in April 1920, which was opened by Margaret McMillan.

The idea of establishing a teachers' training college as a memorial to Margaret McMillan was launched in December 1945 by the then Bishop of Bradford, Dr A. W. F. Blunt. Appeals were made for money, and £110,000 was raised in this way, the remaining nine-tenths of the required amount being provided by the Ministry of Education. A twelve-acre site was bought in Trinity Road in 1949; in 1950 Mrs Attlee cut the first sod, and, with Alderman Kathleen Chambers, she laid the foundation stone in 1952.

Higher education of a different nature was catered for long before the building of 'Mac's', as the college is affectionately known. Bradford's technical college with its domed tower is a landmark, the building opened by the Prince and Princess of Wales on 23 June 1882. Now the technical college and 'Mac's', along with several other constituent colleges which once had separate identity, have been merged into one umbrella organization – Bradford College.

It was the burning ambition of one of the principals of Bradford Technical College to see the establishment of a university in Bradford. This was not achieved until after his retirement, but in November 1966 the opening ceremony was performed and Mr (later Sir) Harold Wilson was installed as Chancellor of the University. The buildings are very fine, especially the library which, in honour of one of Bradford's most famous citizens, has been named the J. B. Priestley Library.

Travelling across the city from the university, one would see wide modern roads which have been built at the cost of demolishing Victorian shops. Much of the building therefore is new, including a block containing the library, The National Museum of Photography, Film and Television and several private concerns; there are also new police headquarters, impressive law courts and the headquarters of a building society, all suitably landscaped. There is the town hall, recently, and unnecessarily, dignified with the appellation 'city hall', and St George's Hall, which rubs shoulders with the ultra-modern, entirely glass, offices of the local newspaper. At the other end of the city from the university, the now stone-washed, sturdy tower of the parish church, elevated to the rank of cathedral, peeps over the roof of the old post office building. A steep hill, Church Bank, up which the trams used to clank and rattle in bygone days, divides the church from Little Germany, and behind it rise several blocks of multi-storey flats, among them Fairfax House and Newcastle House.

The growing nineteenth-century town drew immigrants like a magnet. Some came from fairly local villages and others from other distant parts of the county, while there were also those who came from overseas. Many were Irish who, being Catholic, built churches, of which there are still quite a lot in the city. There were Germans who, over the years, established pork butcher businesses, their own church and many warehouses. Bradford has for a long time been an attractive place for immigrants; after the Second World War there was an influx of workers from Europe, among them Poles and Ukrainians, and, more recently, immigrants from the West Indies, India and Pakistan.

The mills tended to be concentrated in what is known in modern speech as 'the inner city area', and the houses for the workers were built near the mills – this pattern can still be seen notably in the Thornton Road area of the city. It was, of course, in order to get away from this atmosphere of grime and dirt that Titus Salt built his village at Saltaire. The wealthy middle classes did not move so far out: many of them settled in Manningham, where there are still terraces of very fine houses. They show the best features of Victorian architecture, but many of them are in multi-occupation and have become somewhat rundown.

One of the latest acquisitions of the Bradford scene is the Transport Interchange built at the cost of £16.2 million and the envy of transport authorities all over the world. It was opened in March 1977, but its origins reach as far back as the 1930s when the need for a central bus station became apparent, though it was not until 1969 that definite plans began to take shape. It was decided to combine bus and rail stations in a joint terminal, a decision which meant the demise of the old Exchange Station which was opened in 1867.

Architecturally the most striking feature of the Interchange is the 6½-acre canopy roof which comprises eleven thousand panes of reinforced glass and has in excess of a thousand tons of steel girders. In addition to the six enclosed and heated passenger islands and space for sixty-two buses, there is a large underground garage which, at the time of opening, was said to be the biggest man-made cavern in Europe.

The main concourse has developed into a thriving shopping centre with a variety of shops – newsagent, confectioner, greengrocer – which is extremely convenient. And of course the main benefit is that of not having to cross the city centre to catch connections. But it is not to all tastes, having been described by a county councillor as a costly monstrosity built purely to satisfy civic pride.

7

Towns

West Yorkshire has been shaped by manufactures; the old centres of industry, small clustered villages and hamlets, scattered farms and gabled mansions with their mullioned windows, remain on the hills. In the valleys old settlements have expanded; outwards from the church and market-place have spread mills with their rows of cottages for the workers, and mushroom growths have appeared round the bridges where previously there were no settlements. The textile villages, Hunslet, Holbeck, Armley and Bramley, once having separate identity, have been joined to Leeds so that one would never have guessed their former separateness.

The need to feed the factories with wool, cotton and coal and to supply the outside world with finished goods brought into being new systems of transport and improved old ones; roads, canals and railways ran along the valleys, and alongside them more houses, factories and warehouses appeared. Ribbon development took place in the valleys so that the houses of one township almost reached those of the next. Along the valleys of the Aire, the Colne, the Calder, the heavy woollen district and to a less extent in the valleys of the Holme, and the upper Calder and the area between the Aire and Wharfe, this urban sprawl appeared. Other indications of industry are there, the pubs having names linked with the woollen industry, the 'Fleece', 'Woolpack', 'Packhorse', 'Pot o' Four', 'Spinners' Rest', 'Weavers' Arms', to name a few, as well as street names, Tenterfield Terrace, Mill Lane, Mill Street.

Housing developments between the wars bridged any interurban gaps left by nineteenth-century industrialization, while post Second World War developers built outwards, creeping further and further up the hillsides so that the urban spread, like some greedy monster, has gobbled up more and more of the countryside. The towns of the heavy woollen district, particularly, seem to run into one another. Joseph E. Morris in The West Riding of Yorkshire said, 'Nothing can be drearier, or more densely populated, than the region round Dewsbury and Batley.'[1]

In spite of, or perhaps because of, this heavy urbanization, each town has been able to retain, and in most cases is proud to retain, its own identity.

A sort of league table seems attached to town topography, quite different from that used by geographers and town planners to distinguish between hamlet and village, and village and town. A spa town rates highest, evoking visions of eighteenth-century elegance and leisured gentility. A market town comes next, calling to mind a sleepy old-world town where, for six days each week, nothing much happens to disturb the tranquillity. But on one day each week there is scurry and bustle and interest; the whole town comes to life, small knots of people can be seen in the street exchanging news, while the little bow-windowed cafés with their check gingham tablecloths are full of people drinking coffee. A mill town, on the other hand, is definitely down market, drab, possibly dirty, down at heel, while a mining town is the same except more so. Yet market towns have mills, while mill towns and mining towns, too, certainly have markets.

Bingley, 150 years ago, was described as being in a salubrious position, situated between two delightful vales and surrounded by beautiful and well-wooded country, having tolerably well-built houses of brick and stone. A later writer, James Burnley (1875), paid more poetic tribute to the beauty of its environs, painting a prose picture of a town lying 'deep in the shady sadness of a vale'. He soon forgot his lyricism and faced facts, telling us that Bingley was a thriving town hundreds of years ago, when many of the mushroom cities which have sprung up in the last half century were mere obscure hamlets. He spoke of the narrow, undulating main street – the only street – bordered on each side by incongruous buildings. He went on to describe this incongruity – a row or two of stone cottages, tenanted chiefly by factory workers, modern shops with plate-glass windows, more houses and several hostelries. Further down there was an old mansion converted into a bank and, opposite, the new mechanics institute, while further down still was the railway station. He told of the old parish church and of the new church where the incumbent is a 'ritualistic firebrand . . . who froths and fumes and endeavours to frighten the people into penitential exercises'. He then went on to say that the vicar of the parish church – the old church – 'either by virtue of his comfortable doctrines, or by the mere attraction of the ancient church itself, contrives to keep nearly all the best families of the neighbourhood within his fold'.

Although the chapels of the Dissenters were mostly hidden away in back streets and on spaces of waste ground, we are told that the summer weather brought the congregations out into the streets with their hymn books, their ministers and their deacons, where they 'chant a rousing strain and pray with all the vehemence of their lungs'.

He described the leisure-time activities of the townspeople as those of half-witted rustics. During the summer the people of Bingley '. . . when the day's work is over, lounge on the river bridge, go haymaking into the fields, row on the river, watch the canal boats through the locks, loiter about the railway station, ramble through the woods. But, above all, they are fond of indulging in practical jokes. If they can induce a greenhorn to fetch a 'pennorth o' strap oil' from the grocer's, or the second edition of Cock Robin from the bookseller's, their delight is unbounded.'2

Time has wrought change in the century plus since this was written. In 1888 the market hall and cross, and with them the stocks, were moved from their site in the main street to the new Prince of Wales Park where they have since remained. There is at the moment a strong groundswell of opinion which wants to re-site them in the main street, and there is a campaign to achieve this. Main Street has been straightened and widened and new roads have been constructed at right angles to it; a new railway station has been built, a new post office building opened and a free library opened in the mechanics' institute. By the early 1930s Bingley was a busy and self-sufficient little town;

several council schools had joined the national school and the grammar school to provide education, and the town had its own education committee. In a position of eminence, physically, and possibly in the early days also scholastically, was the teachers' training college, opened in 1911. The teaching block with its clock tower surrounded by an arc of five halls of residence was, and still is, an inspiring sight across the valley.

In 1926 the entire building of the old mechanics' institute was handed over to the free library, and Myrtle Grove, a large house standing well on high ground, became the town hall; in fact the whole Myrtle Grove Estate was acquired as a park, Myrtle Park. The council offices were, and still are, housed in the town hall; Bingley does not have, as Wetherby does for instance, and also several other places, a separate town hall and a building for council offices. A new court house and police station came into use in 1929.

Bingley shops were able to supply practically all needs; there was a large weekly market; red buses and trams ran regularly along the main street, and LMS trains, in their maroon and gold livery, steamed up the Aire Valley to Skipton and beyond, and, in the other direction, to Leeds and Bradford. In the summer there were excursion trains to the seaside, Morecambe and Blackpool principally, as it was possible to go through without changing, and, at the appropriate time of the year, half-crown return trips to Morecambe illuminations. Along the canal, flat-bottomed barges brought tons of coal to fuel factory engines and domestic hearths, while in the back streets the hymns of the Dissenters continued to soar heavenwards. In more recent times the town has expanded physically; more and more land is being taken for residential estates to accommodate people who are moving from inner city areas to more rural surroundings.

But the years have diminished the town. It has been merged with a large metropolitan unit, so no longer commands its own affairs; the textile industry has declined and the training college has closed. The apparent inertia of the council after the war prevented Bingley's keeping pace with developments in neighbouring towns. By the time a shopping centre was built, townspeople had formed shopping patterns in other places. There are few West Yorkshire towns with parks as fine as those of

Bingley. At the bottom end of the town is a large park with bowling greens, tennis courts, swings and a stretch of river, while at the other end of the town is a large natural park with moorland and terraced paths. Much could have been done, but has not, to develop tourism, particularly near the river. As a result Bingley is 'summat and nowt of a town'.

So what remains in this town of 'banks, insurance offices and charity shops'? The most attractive way to approach the town is from the Halifax road, from the top of which one sees a panorama of Bingley in the valley below. This view is particularly attractive at night when one can see the lines of lights snaking up and down and across the valley. The road passes the gate of the home of the one-time squire and winds steeply – it is known as 'The Twines' – down to the river, cutting its way through a wood. In spring the woodland is carpeted with bluebells, and there are daffodils round the gate of the baronial residence, while in early summer the estate is ablaze with rhododendrons. Coming into Bingley one passes a pub, the 'Brown Cow', at one end of the bridge, while at the other is the 'White Horse', an extremely attractive white building with stone lanterns on its gables, a building of great age, being at one time in the gift of the Knights of St John. Near the 'White Horse' is the parish church – the old church – a building entirely in proportion and pleasing to the eye. The main road bisects the original graveyard, part of which is now at the other side of the road at the top of a dark and dismal ginnel which leads under the railway to the three rise locks and is known as Treacle Cock Alley.

Approaching from Bradford, one passes, at the top of the town, Bingley's monstrosity, the head offices of the building society, a vast concrete edifice whose ugliness is an affront to the town as well as to the profession of architecture, and a little further down are the Arts Centre and Health Centre set amid attractive and pleasing landscaping well supplied with seats.

Keighley, four miles away higher up the Aire Valley, was, like Bingley, a market town, its chartered market held every Wednesday for five hundred years at the market cross in Church Green, next to the parish church. Like Bingley it grew to prominence as a textile town, but it is bigger and more diverse, having considerable interest in machine-making.

By the 1870s Keighley, after Bradford and Halifax, was the chief seat of the textile trade, having seventy mills devoted to spinning and weaving. Keighley at that time nearly monopolized the trade of making worsted spinning machinery and was also engaged in making looms, for which it gained gold medals at the London and Paris exhibitions of 1862, 1867 and 1878. The first power loom for the manufacture of worsted goods was made in Keighley, and steam-engines were also made there, as well as lathes and machine tools.

Education in Keighley before the Education Act of 1870 owed a great deal to two men, John Drake and Jonas Tonson. In the seventeenth century Drake, an innkeeper, was greatly distressed that there was no encouragement for learning in the town and that for want of knowledge many were seduced by 'that vile sect the Quakers' and others by 'that wicked crew of the Anabaptists' to follow false ways of worship. So worried was he about this that he left a yearly salary for a master of a free school, stipulating that the master should be learned in Latin and Greek and should remain unmarried.

The foundations of the school were laid in 1716, and it was built during the lifetime of Mr Drake, who settled the whole of his estate on it when he died. A lower free school was founded by Jonas Tonson, first built at Exley Head and subsequently transferred to land adjoining Drake's free school. In 1859 a new grammar school was built, and in 1872 the Charity Commissioners, by authority of the Endowed Schools Act of 1869, applied the funds of Drake and Tonson's Trusts to the establishment of a girls' school and towards the support of the trade school in connection with the mechanics' institute.

The girls' department subsequently became Keighley Girls' Grammar School and at some later date was moved to new buildings in Utley, while the trade school became Keighley Boys' Grammar School and continued to function at the mechanics' institute. The girls' school is now comprehensive and functions as a mixed school on the same site, being known as Greenhead Grammar School, Keighley, and the boys' department (also now mixed) functions as a comprehensive school. The founders, Drake and Tonson, are still officially remembered and honoured.

Much of old Keighley has disappeared and there is little to take its place; it has fallen victim to the glass-box architecture which bedevils so much of our city centres at present. Its new shopping centre – level and compact and easy to get about – is open to the sky, saving it from being claustrophobic, as are so many shopping centres recently created in town centres. Delivery to the shops takes place by means of an overhead roadway, which is an unusual and progressive idea as it means that the shopping precinct is entirely and at all times traffic-free.

Coming into Keighley from Skipton, along the tree-lined road, one gets a very favourable impression of a wide and handsome street, and one also passes Cliffe Castle, situated in its own extensive grounds. This is a Victorian Building which was erected by Henry Butterfield of Butterfield Brothers, worsted manufacturers, and it was estimated that he spent £130,000 on building the castle and laying out the grounds. From it there is a glorious view of lower Airedale and the moors beyond. But an even more glorious view of the valley looking north is obtained by walking up the side of the Cliffe Castle Estate, up Spring Gardens Lane as far as the top boundary of the grounds, superb in autumn when one can kick the leaves as one goes. The building and grounds were given to the townspeople of Keighley by Sir Bracewell Smith, who was at one time Lord Mayor of London.

Similarly on the approach from the Bradford side one comes into the town on a tree-lined street and passes one of the town's parks with its large and imposing Leisure Centre. One noteworthy and recent addition is a purpose-built mosque in the streets behind the railway and the main Bradford road. One can catch a glimpse of its minarets from the street end.

The impressive Skipton Road is one of the main thoroughfares; another is Cavendish Street. From the death of Henry Kighley in the latter part of Elizabeth I's reign, the possessions in Keighley descended through the Dukes of Devonshire to Lord George Cavendish who, in 1831, was created Baron Cavendish of Keighley.

Todmorden, like Bingley and Keighley, grew because of industrial expansion. Unlike them, however, it was not an old market town but a place which came into being because indus-

try moved from the hills to the valleys. The modern penchant for
abbreviation, so that Pontefract becomes 'Ponty' and Doncaster
'Donny', produces 'Tod', which is generally acceptable. 'Half to
Tod, please,' 'I'm off down Tod,' are commonly heard expressions. Tod, with a postal designation Todmorden, Lancashire,
has always been in Yorkshire. At one time the Yorkshire/
Lancashire boundary passed through the town hall but in 1888,
for administrative purposes, the town was put into the West
Riding.

Todmorden stands at the junction of three valley routes, one
down the Calder to Halifax, another along the Cliviger Valley
to Burnley, and a third through Littleborough to Rochdale.
Viewed from above, from Stoodley Pike, the town seems to fit
comfortably, one can almost say that it nestles, in a triangle of
land, the widest part of the valley area where the three valleys
converge. Along the three valleys the houses are strung so that
they merge in one direction into the settlements of Cornholme
and Portsmouth and in the other into the village of Walsden.
Looking towards Burnley, one can see a huge red-brick mill and
its attendant chimney and just beyond that Robinwood cotton
mill, a handsome structure – not now used as a cotton mill – and
just beyond it the railway viaduct. On the hillside a prominent
rock formation juts out, just beyond Robinwood Mill; this is
Eagle Rock, and at one time it was the insignia of Robinwood
School. Looking in the other direction, high on the hillside one
can see Dobroyd Castle, once the home of John Fielden, now a
community school, while straight across the valley is the black
tower of Crosstone Church; in the foreground is the railway
viaduct passing through the town centre taking trains to Manchester, the town hall, the graceful spire of the Unitarian
church and the clock tower of St Mary's Church. The houses, in a
mixture of architectural styles, climb the hillside, modern
dwellings and nineteenth-century terrace houses all mixed.

On ground level one can see more: right in the town centre is
the town hall, a noble and interesting building of which the
townspeople are justly and immensely proud. It was built by the
three Fielden brothers, sons of John Fielden of factory reform
fame, at a cost of £54,000, opened on 25 April 1875 and presented to the town by the Fieldens in memory of their father and

uncles. At the front are three semi-circular and concave niches which have no statues in them, but people have wondered if they were originally intended to carry statues of the brothers. The frieze above the pillars is very interesting, portraying the geographical position of the town, representing cotton interests at one side and agricultural interests at the other.

St Mary's Church stands at the junction of the three valleys facing east. The original building was erected between 1400 and 1476 and because of its convenient situation was attended by the people of Stansfield and Langfield townships. But by an Act of 1866 Christ Church, a short distance away, was designated the parish church, and St Mary's became a chapel of ease. Todmorden's first school was built under the shadow of St Mary's – the 'endowed school', which is still there, although not now used as a school. Its founder was Richard Clegg, the vicar of Kirkham, who was the grandson of Richard Clegg of Stonehouse Walsden. It was stipulated that the schoolmaster was to be elected by a majority of the freeholders of Todmorden and Walsden. The schoolhouse was in the parsonage garden and consisted of a schoolroom for a hundred scholars with a dwelling-house for the master; the children's playground was at the back of the church.

Also near the town centre is Todmorden Hall, which served for many years as the post office and is now a restaurant. The present building was erected by Savile Radcliffe early in the seventeenth century, and some of the timbers of an earlier, medieval building remain in the present one. The walls of what was once the drawing-room are of panelled oak, and there is a fine oak mantelpiece on which the arms of the Radcliffe family are carved.

At the other side of the town is Stansfield Hall, once the residence of another prominent family who, however, left the district in the seventeenth century, and later the residence of Joshua Fielden. While, in the Civil War, the Stansfields supported Parliament, the Radcliffes and the Crossleys, who lived at Scaitcliffe Hall, further along the valley and now an old people's home, were ardent Royalists. This particular district, below the golf course, is one of the nicest parts of the town, with some superb detached houses.

Hebden Bridge is, arguably, the most interesting town in West Yorkshire. Originally the bridge with its mill was the place to which farmers on the hillsides brought their corn to be ground. This was not so much because of the impossibility of doing it at home as because there was an obligation on tenants to grind their corn at the manorial mill and pay for the privilege of doing so. The clothiers also brought their pieces down to the fulling mill, and eventually, with the increased use of water power in textiles, and later of steam power, mills and houses grew in the valleys and a settlement developed at the bridge over Hebden Water.

The bridge, built in 1510, and the mill remain in the centre of the town, and from it a packhorse track climbs steeply up the hill to Heptonstall. Higher up the town from the old bridge is a newer one, wide enough to carry a road, while lower is another bridge which takes the traffic up the valley to Todmorden and to Lancashire. The roads over the bridges are, apart from the town streets, the only level roads in Hebden Bridge, for all the other ways from the town, both old and new, climb steeply. Overhead in the town was a remark, 'All t' best legs come from Hebden Bridge.' Just what was intended by the remark one will never know, but with hills to climb on the scale of the Calder Hills, there is no wonder Hebden legs are strong.

The physical lay-out of the place is endlessly fascinating. A. Wainwright, whose pictorial guides to the Lakeland Fells and guides to long-distance walks are extremely popular, has, in his *Pennine Way Companion* (1965–7), likened it to a Tibetan monastery. The terraces of houses on the level land are built so that every bit of space is used, while the hillside houses seem to be clinging there, being built literally into the hillside, with more storeys at one side than the other. An excellent viewpoint of the houses is from the Heptonstall road, while another is from the Horse Hold Road at the other side of the valley. Hebden Bridge is a busy, bustling town but not any more with the throb of machinery. At one time it was a thriving textile town; since the decline in the demand for textile goods the factories have closed and the town has turned more to tourism, which has grown, along with an influx of residents from other parts of the country. Many of the local people cannot understand the attraction the place has, and while mourning its demise as a working town, they accept the trend to tourism as a regrettable alternative.

At the other side of the county, where the River Wharfe divides West from North Yorkshire, manufacturing industry scarcely impinged. Otley, although a busy town, grew to prominence as a market centre rather than a mill town.

An early nineteenth-century writer seemed to damn with faint praise when he wrote that Otley was 'pleasantly situated on the banks of the Wharfe but is a small town and does not contain anything that merits particular notice. It however, particularly attracts the attention of a traveller from its romantic appearance and the beauty of its surrounding fields and meadows. A craggy cliff hangs over the town which seems to threaten it with immediate destruction but on arriving at the summit the variety of objects that present themselves are truly enchanting.'[3] One is not of course clear about the exact nature of the objects which presented themselves – they will probably have disappeared by now; or the writer may have meant the view, which is magnificent.

The most spectacular way of coming into Otley by road from West Yorkshire is from Leeds, where suddenly one sees a wide and extensive view of lower Wharfedale and, looking the other way, the rocky promontory of Almscliffe Crag. The 'craggy cliff' is on the left.

The craggy cliff is, of course, Otley Chevin, which dominates the town. It is 925 feet above sea level, and its name is derived from the Celtic *kefn* which means a ridge. The Chevin was enclosed in 1779, and now most of its rocks are hidden in tall plantations; some have been split and used for building purposes, blocks of stone being sent from the Chevin to form the foundations of the Houses of Parliament. Every year in Holy Week, there is a cross on the Chevin and, standing out against the skyline in the often sombre weather which is common at the time of year, it is a fitting reminder of the Good Friday story. Otley is in a fortunate position to be able to do this; although many of the West Yorkshire towns are surrounded by hills, none could show the cross in this dramatic way.

The parish church, which is in the centre of the town, is a large substantial building. The first church in Otley was built by Edwin of Northumbria after the bringing of Christianity to the north of England by Paulinus in AD 627. The bulk of the present building is probably Decorated, and the oldest part Norman. In the south transept is a carved memorial to Thomas, Lord Fairfax, and Helen Aske, his lady, who was descended from the Cliffords of Skipton Castle; they were the grandparents of Sir Thomas Fairfax, the friend of Oliver Cromwell, famous in the Civil War.

Facing Manor Square is the Free Grammar School which was founded in 1611 and named Prince Henry's Grammar School in honour of the then Prince of Wales, who conferred upon the trustees the honour of a corporate body. The motto was 'Fear God and Mind Thy Book'. The founder was Thomas Cave of Wakefield who had been a travelling salesman or packman for many years and who had amassed a moderate fortune and wished to leave some of it for the children of the people among whom he had traded. The present grammar school is not in this building but in newer and bigger premises.

The Manor House is a Georgian building which was supposedly designed by Mr Carr who built Harewood House, and it was originally intended that the house should be built further up the river. The wife of the man for whom it was being built, however, wanted it to be where she should see up Kirkgate, and when her husband was away on business, she had the pegs removed, the foundations dug on the present site and the building under course of construction by the time he got back.

Otley is a very pleasant town with a thriving market, and it attracts a great many tourists. Its main street, Boroughgate, is perpetually busy as it is the main thoroughfare to Harrogate.

The name of Thomas Chippendale is associated with Otley; in fact the premises once occupied by the Free Grammar School have been acquired by the Sam Chippendale foundation. Surprisingly little is known about Thomas Chippendale. An early work claimed that he was a native of Worcestershire who, on going to London, found work as a joiner, but a document of 1770, which was published at a later date, linked Thomas Chippendale, cabinet-maker, with a William Chippendale of Otley, Yorkshire, and an entry in the parish church registers records for 5 June 1718 the baptism of Thomas Chippendale, son of John Chippendale of Otley, 'Joyner'.

It seems that he started work with his father in Otley and that soon his genius was recognized by the Lascelles family of Harewood House. He also had connections with Nostell Priory. At some point in his life Chippendale went to London, possibly to study drawing and design. There is a record of his marriage on 19 May 1748, when he was about thirty, his bride being Catherine Redshaw, about whom nothing is known beyond the fact that she came from the parish of St Martin's. She bore him eleven children and died in 1772, following which he remained a widower for five years and in 1777 married Elizabeth Davis at Fulham parish church. He was buried in November 1779 at St Martin in-the-Fields.

Whether he carried on his business from his residence or at a separate workshop is not clear, but it was a large and flourishing business in which he employed at least twenty-two craftsmen. In August 1754 he acquired a partner, and in 1755 an insurance policy was taken out covering a total sum of £3,700. In 1760 he was elected a member of the Society for the Encouragement of Arts, Manufactures and Commerce, being proposed by a fellow Yorkshireman. His partner, James Rannie, died in 1766, and in order that the estate should be settled, the stock of furniture and timber was offered for sale. The sale notice makes clear that the firm were makers of furniture, kept in stock a supply of feathers for stuffing mattresses and also sold carpets. In addition they carried a supply of ready-made articles for those who did not wish to have furniture made from a special pattern. In 1771 another partner was admitted. Correspondence reveals Chippendale was a hard-working man whose business meant that he had to do a certain amount of travelling about the country and also abroad.

Several miles higher up Wharfedale is Ilkley, famous in its time as a Roman town and later as a health spa. There are probably few of its many visitors who would know much about its history, simply regarding it as a place for a pleasant summer afternoon. Few, too, think of it as anything but a town, although it remained a village for some time after the medicinal properties of its waters had been recognized. A guide-book of 1829 describes it as a neat little village.

The cold spring which gushed out of the hill with great force was thought to be of benefit to those suffering from scorbutic and cutaneous diseases. (Scorbutic disorders were those associated with scurvy, and cutaneous diseases were skin diseases.) Bathing in these waters was in great demand especially in the summer, for pleasure as well as health. Householders were not slow to take advantage of what nature had bounteously provided, and already in 1829 there were six boarding-houses, thirty lodging-houses, and three inns, the 'Rose and Crown', the 'Wheatsheaf' and the 'Listers Arms'. The bath-house contained two baths of equal dimensions, each holding 1,160 gallons of water and taking thirteen minutes to fill. A man and his wife acted as attendants and were described as very attentive. There was a sitting-room provided so that those who were waiting their turn to bathe could rest in comfort, and there was stabling for the asses. For of course the baths were out of the village and many of those attending there would be aged or infirm, or both and, for their convenience, it was possible to hire asses for transport. 4d. seems to have been the going rate for transport from the village to the wells, and there were several firms who had animals for hire. Between five and eight in the morning was the best time to arrive, and people were warned about going in wet weather when the path was likely to be extremely slippery. Water was also provided for drinking; it was not thought to have many medicinal qualities as a beverage, but it was cold and refreshing.

It was evident that Ilkley was establishing itself as a holiday resort, as several firms in addition to supplying asses to the wells advertised them for hire on a weekly or even an hourly basis. Some had four- or two-wheeled donkey carriages for hire at 8d. or 9d. an hour.

In order to bring people to the town of Ilkley from outside, the Defiance coach ran between Ilkley and Leeds in the season. Its route was Ilkley, Burley, Otley, Leeds, and of course in reverse. It ran on Mondays and Tuesdays at 7 a.m. and on Thursdays and Saturdays at 8 a.m., returning the same evening, the outside fare being 3s. and the inside 5s.

By the mid 1860s Ilkley had acquired an air of prosperity and was referred to as a parish town, consisting of a main street leading east to west with two others intersecting a different points, one leading north, the other south. Many houses in the lower part of the town were described as old, retaining their primitive thatch. It appeared, however, that a spirit of progress was about as there were plans to remove them. In the meantime rows of elegant-looking private lodging-houses with light, airy rooms had been built, many enjoying beautiful prospects with pretty gardens in front. These were in the higher parts of the town on the edge of the moor.

Ilkley was really developing as a tourist centre with, during the season, abundant tea-, coffee- and eating-rooms. It was also possible to hire carriages and and horses at reasonable rates at almost any hour. The number of hotels had also increased; there was the 'Crescent', the 'Listers Arms', the 'Rose and Crown', the 'Albion', the 'Star' and the Station Hotel – because of course much of the development of the town was due to its having a railway which made it much more accessible.

In addition to these there were several hydropathic establishments. Ben Rhydding had one which was described in *Guide to Ilkley* 1865 as follows: 'The building is a large and picturesque fabric in the Scottish baronial style of architecture.' Standing on a terrace above the town was Ilkley Wells House, while Craiglands and the Troutbeck were also hydropathic establishments.

The increased accessibility of Ilkley because of the railway was reflected in its growth of popularity as a health and holiday resort, but it also, because of its rail link, developed as a dormitory town for the wool magnates of Bradford and Leeds. Ilkley is now largely a residential and tourist town.

Whatever description can be applied to most West Yorkshire towns, 'gracious' is not one of them, although there is one town to which this word applies and that is Boston Spa. Like Todmorden, Hebden Bridge and many of the mining villages, it was a place of mushroom growth but for vastly different reasons. The spring was accidentally discovered in 1744 by a labourer named John Shires who was cutting brushwood on the banks of the river. He constantly drank draughts of the water, but whether this practice contributed to his longevity or not – he lived to be eighty – we do not know. In 1784 the water was submitted to a series of experiments. Fresh from the spring it had a limpid, sparkling appearance, a saline taste and a sulphurous smell. As a result of this discovery, the village rapidly developed from mere countryside to a flourishing town. By 1853 there were 250 houses, most of them extremely elegant, built of stone from the Clifford Moor Quarry.

A Guidebook of 1853 tells of the pure and bracing air to be experienced at Boston Spa, where one might bathe in the beneficial waters or drink them, there being a pump room, good accommodation and a variety of baths. There were some commodious inns and a variety of respectable lodging-houses as well as good shops with civil and obliging shopkeepers. In addition there were fertile gardens which produced a plentiful supply of fruit, vegetables and flowers. It was, however, to be regretted that there were few facilities for entertainment, although there was hunting during the season and also fishing. One scarcely expects people in need of the benefits of health-giving baths to be in a fit state to indulge in hunting and fishing. However, the guidebook continued with the attractions of the spa – there was a circulating library and a news room, and the place abounded in delightful walks, while occasionally there were entertainments from pupils of the Yorkshire School for the Blind.

Boston Spa, although it no longer functions as a spa town, is extremely pleasant. Its main street is busy as the traffic whizzes through; some of the gracious, elegant houses which were built in its heyday as a spa are still there, and it is an extremely popular place for fishing.

An unlikely place for a spa town is Slaithwaite in the Colne valley, but at one time it was noted far and wide for the excellence of its mineral springs and baths in the spa grounds; it was even thought that the mineral virtue of the water equalled that of Harrogate. The name Slaithwaite – originally Slaugh-Thwaite or Slaighthwaite – is derived from the 'slaugh' or sloe tree, as apparently at one time these were prolific in the neighbourhood. In common with much of the country in Calderdale, with which it has a physical affinity, it is probable that at one time it was possible for a squirrel to jump from tree to tree all the way from Marsden to Huddersfield.

Until just over a hundred years ago the ancient church in Slaithwaite was the only one for the four townships of Slaith-

waite and Golcar in Huddersfield parish and Lingard and Linth-
waite in Almondbury parish. Quite a pleasant little town, it has
now no evidence of activity as a spa, and in common with much
of the rest of the county has suffered from the slump in the
textile industries. The pronunciation of the name is confusing
not only to outsiders but also to local people. 'Slaithwaite' –
pronounced as it is written, is not used, the vernacular being
'Slowitt' or 'Slathwaite'. British Rail, when about to open their
station there recently, had no idea which form to use for their
loudspeaker announcements. Accordingly they appealed to local radio for arbitration, and even among local people there
seemed to be almost equal support for each form.

The development of mining and spread of railways in the
south part of the county brought about the rapid development of
some of the farming villages. Hemsworth, for instance, was a
farming village which derived its name from the great quantity
of hemp which was grown and manufactured in the neighbourhood. The directory of 1822 showed a population of 963, and
included in it were a few victuallers and a scattering of the
miscellaneous occupations necessary for the maintenance of life
in an agricultural village.

Hemsworth is well known for the foundation of the Holgate
Hospital and the Holgate Grammar School. Robert Holgate, the
fifty-ninth Archbishop of York, who was probably a native of
Hemsworth and who died in 1555, endowed a hospital and a
grammar school there. The hospital was intended to provide a
home for ten poor men and ten poor women of Hemsworth and
three other parishes, and was to be under the supervision of a
master who was to be a clerk in Holy Orders. In 1857 the Court
of Chancery drew up a new scheme for the administration of the
hospital after which the present master's house, chapel and
almshouses were built. The quadrangle system at Oxford and
Cambridge inspired the plan, although in the end the cottages
were built only on two sides.

The trust is still financed solely from the endowment of Robert
Holgate, and the inmates are still known as brothers and
sisters, receiving àn annual sum of £40 each. Some moderniz-
ation of the cottages has been done, central heating has been
installed and attractive modern bathrooms put in. An alarm

bell has been fitted which rings in the master's house and in the establishment of the porter. Even as late as 1966 the uniform knee-length coats for men and the stuff gowns for women were still worn by the pensioners in chapel, but these have now fallen out of use. Although the master must be a clerk in Holy Orders, there is no restriction on the denomination of the pensioners. The minimum age to qualify for entry is sixty.

The fluctuating fortunes of the grammar school led to the endowment being transferred to Barnsley, and a new grammar school was eventually opened at Hemsworth in 1921.

In the mid 1860s the Wakefield to Doncaster railway line was opened, and in the 1880s the Barnsley to Hull line, both serving the Hemsworth area; towards the end of the nineteenth century the rich Barnsley Main seam of coal was opened: it was these events which developed Hemsworth, and the village grew into a mining town. Today it is a busy place with roads to Wakefield, Doncaster, Pontefract and Barnsley humming with constant traffic.

At the top end of the town, on an eminence, is the church, with a plain tower and no turrets, standing in a suitably patriarchal position. Lower down is a landscaped sloping garden with seats, known as Crosshill. With its rows of red-brick houses, Hemsworth has no pretensions to graciousness and no stately buildings.

Castleford, situated near the confluence of the Aire and the Calder, was another village which was developed by mining and industry. It is no surprise to find that the rivers in the eighteenth century were the haunt of salmon, trout and grayling, nor to learn that,

> Castleford lasses might well be fair
> For they wash in Calder and rinse in Aire.

In the eighteenth century Castleford consisted of a few streets; at the beginning of the nineteenth century its population was 793, and at the beginning of the twentieth century 17,386.

The pottery industry has existed in Castleford since the Middle of the seventeenth century; the Directory of 1822, however, listed only two potmakers, while it listed twenty-one vessel-owners, the largest single occupation in the lists. In 1826 the Aire and Calder Navigation began the construction of a canal to Goole, and when it was completed, a regular service of boats plied with passengers and goods between Castleford and Goole. There was also a coach which ran from the Ship Inn to meet the stage-coaches on the Great North Road to Ferrybridge. In 1829 the glass bottle industry was introduced and in 1864 the chemical industry, while 1868 saw the start of Wheldale collieries, after which there was an influx of miners. Subsequently other pits were opened in the neighbourhood, and the village grew into a town.

A town completely unspoilt by industry is Wetherby which is situated on the Great North Road at a point nearly midway between London and Edinburgh. In the eighteenth century it was a notable stopping-place for mail coaches, and so of course inns abounded, two of the most famous being, at that time, the 'Angel' and the 'Swan and Talbot'. The 'Angel' was a large inn which had stable room for upwards of a hundred horses, and forty pairs of horses were regularly kept there for posting purposes. In 1810 the chambermaid at the 'Angel' had to pay £70 a year for the right of her situation and also had to pay £10 10s. a year to her maid, while the waiter had to pay £30 per year to his master, pay his man out of his own pocket and give security of £80 for the silver plate in his care.

In the centre of Wetherby is the market-place, in which stands the town hall, built on the site of the old Chapel of Ease, the foundation stone laid on 11 June 1845. A day school for boys and girls was held in the lower rooms of the hall, their playground being the open street. The November hirings for the girls were held in the schools, and the children were given a holiday for the occasion. Election-day speeches were given from the open windows and the steps of the town hall. An old election story is told that every man who entered the inn in Cross Street had his hat snatched off his head and thrown on the fire, later to be replaced by a new one at the candidate's expense.

What seems to have impressed nineteenth-century visitors was the bridge, the river and the weir: 'Wetherby is a small well built market town pleasantly situated on the River Wharfe over which it has a noble bridge above which the river forms a

beautiful cascade by falling in a grand sheet of water over a high
dam erected for the convenience of the mills where they not only
grind corn but press great quantities of oil from rape seed and
rasp log wood for the use of the clothiers and dyers.'[4]

8

Villages

The dictionary definition of a village as 'an assemblage of houses smaller than a town' is perhaps technically correct, but it is unsatisfying and remote from the average person's concept of a village. Small, compact, rural, pretty, complete – a village needs to be all these and more besides. It must harmonize with its surroundings so that it appears to have grown from them. Its buildings, although not displaying the uniformity which is characteristic of mass production, must be sufficiently similar to show the unity of a common interest. Such is the village scene, set in the heart of rural England, for which men fought and died in two world wars and whose picture, representing home, sustained them through many weary hours.

Some villages remain apparently little touched by the passage of time, like Woolley and Wragby, while in others it is difficult to distinguish the old core of the village from the mass of new building which has taken place. In yet others new building has taken place on the edge of the old settlement so that physically the old village stands surrounded, or fringed, by new housing estates, giving the appearance of two distinct settlements.

Four villages whose recent history has followed this pattern lie on the north-east side of Leeds. Thorner has some outlying farms and cottages and a long main street with most attractive houses along both sides of it. They are stone-built, sufficiently different to show individuality but yet similar, many of them having woodwork which is painted white, and shutters, decorative rather than functional. Thorner is a village, surrounded by undulating farming land. Bramham stands on the Great North Road where once stage-coaches rolled past and droves of ani-

mals plodded their way north or south. More recently its dangerous crossroad was an accident blackspot to be replaced by a
flyover. Edmund Bogg (a prolific writer of topographical books
about Yorkshire between 1891 and 1926) thought the village
with the red-tiled roofs in the older portion, contrasting with the
grey slated roofs of the later buildings, had a Continental,
rather Flemish, appearance.

A mile from Bramham is Clifford, and another mile further on
is Thorp Arch. Clifford is a picturesque village which in the
nineteenth century was a thriving place having flax mills. So
many Irish immigrants came to work there that a Roman
Catholic church was built, an impressive building in the Norman style. There is also a Protestant church which is unusual as
one would not expect so small a place to be able to maintain two
churches of major denominations.

Whereas Wragby has kept its original appearance and its
function as a farming village, other villages in the mining area
in the south part of the county have mushroomed in the last
hundred years. In Walton the new housing has almost sub-
merged the core of the old village, while at Crofton the stone
church in the trees seems to have little relevance to the rest of
the village. Kinsley and Fitzwilliam were created by the coal-
mining industry and the railway, and Sharlston, Ryhill and
South Hiendley have developed from farming villages into
fairly big mining communities.

The contrast so marked in other aspects of the West Yorkshire
scene is evident in the villages on the borders of the county. In
the north-west at the head of the Cliviger Valley are the twin
villages of Cornholme and Portsmouth which run into one another so that it is difficult to know where one ends and the other
begins. The Cliviger Valley is narrow, rather gorge-like and impressive, and one could quite understand anyone travelling
through it on a dismal, misty day feeling awed and threatened by
the high, bleak hills. Cornholme and Portsmouth are creations
of industrial expansion when, in the 1880s, families moved
from the hillside farms to work in the mills. They consist almost
entirely of streets of terraced houses, some placed parallel to
the valley, others at right angles to it. Modern housing, consisting of blocks of flats, occupies the site of a former bobbin mill –

hence its name, Bobbin Mill Close; the bobbin mill at one time dominated the village, being the major place of employment.

The hills enclosing the valley are steep and bare, with rough grass, bracken and frequent outcrops of Millstone Grit, while on the lower slopes there are patches of green pastureland. Clinging tenaciously to the hillside are slender, hardy trees with here and there small patches of woodland, and these, in spring and autumn, soften the grimness of the hillsides. Although some of the houses have been stone washed by the Department of the Environment, many have not and their blackness, especially those in the streets built transversely and crowded into the narrowest part of the valley, lend a dark and claustrophobic atmosphere. Industry, as well as formal religion, has declined in recent years, and many of the mills have been pulled down. A Methodist chapel has recently been demolished, leaving only its graveyard as a reminder of the faith of our fathers, for Nonconformity was strong in this part of industrial West Yorkshire. There is an Anglican church still, and also a Baptist chapel. The streets names are not inspiring: Ernest Street, Spring Street, Blackrock Street, which seems apt, Roseberry Terrace, Gladstone Street and Victoria Terrace give some indication of age.

At the turn of the century many never left the village; there were no buses, although the valley had a railway, and the village a station. The many and varied shops supplied all material needs, and the church – of the Established and Dissenting varieties – provided plenty of social life. There was the Mothers' Union, the Band of Hope, the succession of At Homes, Women's Weekends, Young Ladies' Weekends and Men's Weekends, by which the chapel calendar was marked. And for those who had no taste for religion, even in its social form, there was the 'Waggon and Horses', the Liberal Club and the Working Men's Club. Although the railway still runs through the valley and some passenger trains still operate, the village no longer has a station. There are precious few shops, and so villagers now use the half-hourly bus service either down the valley to Todmorden or over the border to Burnley.

The Walsden Valley, going out to Lancashire from the other end of Todmorden, is softer, gentler and somewhat less rugged than the Cliviger Valley, and it flattens out more gradually as

one reaches the border. The language leaves one in no doubt as
to *which* border: 'Top o' th' close' is the name of a road, and 'Bird
i' th' hand' is the name of a pub. But it is the same type of terrain,
grassy moorland and rough grazing land dotted with isolated
trees and here and there small clusters of woodland. Black stone
walls broken in places cross the fellsides, and here and there is a
dilapidated cottage. Outcrops of black Millstone Grit abound,
and at one side of the valley there is the artificial mound of
Summit Tunnel with its round airshafts. An unwary visitor
could not believe her eyes as she saw clouds of steam issuing
from the bowels of the earth and erupting in front of her.

The buildings along the valley display a mixture of styles:
there are clustered farms hugging the hillside, some eighteenth
century, some nineteenth, built in traditional style and blending with the landscape, and rows of nineteenth-century cottages, one of them cheek by jowl with a chalet-style bungalow.
Further down the valley modern bungalows and red-brick
houses are mixed with traditional black stone houses, while on
the Walsden industrial estate there are modern mills in simu-
lated corrugated material; several blocks of high-rise flats complete the ill-assorted jumble. Right in the heart of the streets is
St Peter's Church, a graceful building, with a long, slender
spire, lifting one's soul and spirit to the hills.

Walsden is a community which grew out of the Industrial
Revolution; previously the settlement was scattered. A survey
of 1626 lists seventeen freeholders and ten copyholders; they
farmed the land, grazing animals on Inchfield Common and
combining farming with textile work or possibly metal working,
as in Ramsden Clough there is evidence of bloomeries.

In 1804 a cotton mill was built at Clough near Walsden, and in
1813 a few inhabitants erected a school (Lanebottom) on land
given to them by John Fielden of Bottomley. The trust deed said
that they were desirous of establishing a Sunday School at
Bottomley for instructing the children of the poor and indigent
in reading, writing and arithmetic. The trustees were authorized to permit a person or persons as they saw fit to preach a
sermon from time to time on Sundays, and as nothing was laid
down about denomination, the sermons were preached by members of the Established Church and also Methodists. Under the

1870 Education Act the school was transferred to the management of the School Board.

The buildings of the two villages, many of them blackened by the grime of a century, are part of a heritage and, as such, should never have been stone-washed. Villages like Cornholme and Walsden have engendered a real sense of community among those who live there; there is a warm-hearted friendliness which is characteristic of the whole area. One woman, who had lived at Cornholme until she had married, when she moved to Walsden said she found that there she was regarded as 'an off cumed 'un'. But, referring to the entire area, she said she wouldn't, couldn't, live anywhere else: it was 'just like one big happy family'.

Moving right across the county to the border with South Yorkshire, one might expect to find a different sort of village. Travelling along the road from Notton towards Woolley crossroads, it is easy to imagine oneself in the heart of a rural community instead of between two major conurbations. Fields stretch as far as the eye can see, in the foreground cows graze, and beyond, the ripening barley waves in the breeze. Only on the far southern skyline can a clue be detected as to nearby industry, for the buildings on the skyline are those of Barnsley.

Over the tops of the trees can be seen the tower of Woolley church, but no other part of the village is visible from the Notton Road. In Anglo-Saxon times the whole area was thickly wooded and in the forests lurked wolves, prevalent until the thirteenth century – in fact the name means a forest glade frequented by wolves. By the time of Domesday, Woolley was a sizeable settlement.

Visually Woolley is extremely pleasing, being a clustered village, unlike its neighbour Notton which is a straggling village with a large and rather sprawling village green. In Notton there has been a lot of modern house building, whereas in Woolley modern development is discreetly hidden at the back of the village. Woolley's grouped houses give the impression of a closely knit entity, and there is a large, although compact, village green presided over by a big sycamore tree, while at the top end of the green is a playing-field with swings and at the corner the small village school. The other sides of the green are overlooked by fine old houses built of stone, dating mostly from the early eighteenth to the early nineteenth century. The church lies at the back of the village, and up the lane leading to it are farms and cottages, three of the farms having names of trees, Beech Farm, Ash Farm and Pear Tree Farm. Woolley boasts a High Street and a Finkle Street.

The discerning visitor who comes to Woolley with no fore-knowledge can find several clues to explain it: the absence of any place of worship other than an Anglican church, the general tidiness of the place, the presence of Woolley Hall further down the road. Woolley is, or was, until 1949, an estate village. Woolley Hall was the home of the Wentworths, of whom one, the well-known Thomas, Earl of Strafford, was Lord Deputy of Ireland in the reign of Charles I and famous, along with his contemporary, Archbishop Laud, for his policy of 'thorough'. The Wentworths came to Woolley in 1599, when Michael Wentworth bought the hall which was eventually replaced in 1635, and the family remained there until after the Second World War. The Hall is now a college for adult education. Ownership of the village was at one time shared between several families of freeholders, but by the nineteenth century the entire village had passed to the Wentworths.

The economy of the village is, and has been, agricultural; a directory of 1822 listed, in addition to the square and clergy, a wheelwright, a victualler, a butcher, three farmers and two maltsters. Now, however, because of its position, five miles from Wakefield and five from Barnsley, it is ideal for commuters. There is no indication in the village of the vast mineral wealth existing underground and which was discovered in the mid-nineteenth century under the Woolley Estate. Only a sign saying 'Woolley Colliery' – some way from the village – indicates the presence of coalfields.

About as far away from Woolley as it is possible to be and still be in West Yorkshire is another border village with which it has spiritual links. It too is an estate village where Nonconformity has not set an official foot; it has a village green and also links with the Wentworth family.

Thorp Arch has been described as one of the most delightful spots in the lower valley of the Wharfe, and this is not inapt. The traditional village forms a complete whole, although naturally it falls into two sections, one consisting of the houses grouped round the village green and the other of the houses along the village street, and this division is perpetuated by the GPO: letters to the former are addressed to 'so and so, The Green, Thorp Arch', and the latter, 'The Village', with the number of the house. The cottages are of stone, the light sandstone of which much of York is built, giving the buildings a creamy hue and blending with the agricultural background of the area. There has been modern private development which is discreet and blends well with the older cottages.

Approaching from Wetherby, one reaches 'The Village' first and from Boston Spa, 'The Green'. Coming from Boston Spa, one crosses the River Wharfe over a bridge designed for single-line traffic. There are triangles in the side of the parapet for the safety of foot passengers, although there are no traffic lights so that one adopts a sort of gentleman's agreement for driving across the bridge, which seems to work.

Thorp Arch was in the gift of Osbern de Arches who was High Sheriff of Yorkshire in 1100. At the time of Domesday Book there was a priest and a church, which was probably Saxon, later to be followed by a Norman church; the archway of the Norman porch is there and also the foundations. In the fifteenth century the church was rebuilt in the Perpendicular style, and in 1756 it underwent almost a complete demolition and rebuilding.

At one time the estate had connections with the Wentworth family but eventually it came into the hands of the Hastings family. Lady Elizabeth Hastings, perhaps the best-known member of the family, was born in 1682. Through her mother she succeeded to considerable property, and the death of her brother George meant that she succeeded in 1704–5 to the family estate at Ledston Park near Pontefract, which became her permanent residence. As a young woman she was very beautiful and graceful; she never married but devoted her life and considerable wealth to works of piety and charity; charities throughout England were to benefit, and the church in Thorp Arch was one of them.

She left a sum of £14 each year to provide bread and wine for a monthly sacrament in Thorp Arch church. There was also £100 for beautifying or rebuilding the chancel and new paving for the church and for a covering for the Communion table, for a pulpit cloth and cushion all in purple material, and for building a gallery for the children of the charity school who attended church. Another gallery or seats was to be provided in place of those taken out of the chancel. Lady Elizabeth also left sufficient money for a silver chalice, paten and flagon to be used at Holy Communion, and a sum of £5 every twenty years for beautifying the church. The charity school from which the children were to come to church was also instituted by her, and for this she endowed the yearly sum of £15 for the schoolmaster, in addition to the lands belonging to the schoolhouse. The vicar of Thorp Arch received an annual sum of £2 in order to buy school books, English books and tracts being specified as the most suitable.

She laid down that the number of children to be taught in the school should be twenty, and in the event of there not being twenty poor children, the number should be made up out of the neighbouring villages; all were to be taught to read, write and cost accounts. Lady Elizabeth was nothing if not practical, and she was anxious to encourage ambition as she stipulated that the lessons taught should be of use so that those who wished to progress from being farmers' servants to farmers themselves should benefit.

In winter, when the days were short and there was often bad weather, she realized that there would be times when it was too bad for the children to attend. In this case the necessary number of twenty could be made up from adults, Lady Elizabeth hoping that even housekeepers who were unhappy enough not to have been taught in their youth would not be ashamed to attend for instruction. She did not, and possibly could not, envisage a time when education would be provided by the state.

The school, although not the building, still exists, and it embraces a far wider sample of population than the poor, a greater number than twenty and a far wider range of subjects than reading, writing and casting accounts. The school is known as 'The Lady Elizabeth Hastings School'; the trustees are still responsible for the upkeep of the fabric of the school, and the children have sweatshirts with the school's title printed on them.

In 1982 the three-hundredth anniversary of the birth of Lady Elizabeth Hastings was celebrated, and the children showed their prowess. The infants gave a display of swimming, one class played rounders, and inside the school other children played board games of the sort which would have been popular three hundred years ago. There were gymnastic and dancing displays, including maypole dancing and instrumental music, the recorder-players wearing seventeenth-century costume.

Thorp Arch is a peaceful agricultural village, despite the plethora of penal establishments on its periphery. (In Thorp Arch there is a Remand Centre, an Open Prison and a Community School, in nearby Wetherby a Borstal, while at Askham Richard, which is in North Yorkshire, there is an Open Prison for Women.) During the Second World War an enormous ordnance factory was opened there, and after the war it was converted to a huge trading estate which draws vast crowds of people, especially at weekends.

Approaching Skipton from the south, one sees a fairly nondescript, but not unpleasing, cluster of houses on a spur of land overlooking the Aire Gap. This small community is in fact not one village but two, although no obvious boundary presents itself either on the ground or on a map, but boundary there is. In the south it follows a stream and then takes a rather arbitrary line across heather moorland. These two villages, Kildwick and Farnhill, were divided by the planners who framed the 1974 Local Government Act, Farnhill being put into North Yorkshire and Kildwick into West.

Coming from West Yorkshire, one approaches the village across a fine bridge, a monument to the open-handedness of the canons of Bolton Priory by whom it was built, or perhaps rebuilt, in the reign of Edward I in 1305 or 1306, at a cost of £21. 12s. 9d., and it is the oldest bridge over the River Aire of which any written record exists. The present structure consists of two pointed and two rounded arches and was originally only about half its present width. The widening which took place in 1780 has greatly destroyed its ancient appearance.

At the bottom of the village stands the church; there was one on the site in Saxon times which was later replaced by a Norman church. Some destruction to the fabric was caused by the Scots who invaded the district in 1317, but just how much depredation can be laid at their door is uncertain, and it is likely that they were mollified by the fact that the church is dedicated to St Andrew. The tower and parts of the nave and aisles were probably restored in the fourteenth century, and further renewal took place about the beginning of the sixteenth century, when the present choir was added in perpendicular Gothic. The church was extended to an unusual length and was named 'the Lang Kirk o' Craven'; it is 145½ feet long and 48½ feet wide, including the aisles. It stands well, as if guarding the two villages, yet at the same time welcoming strangers and travellers. From the top gate of the church a flagged path, known locally as Parson's Walk, connects it to the one-time vicarage and the hall.

The village and manor of Kildwick were given to the Priory of Embsay by Cecilia de Romillé, the daughter of a Norman noble to whom the Conqueror had given large estates in Craven; at a later date the priory was moved to Bolton. At Kildwick the canons established a grange, no doubt for sheep-rearing; it is still there, between Kildwick and Silsden, standing a little way back from the road which is known officially as Grange Road but unofficially as 'the top road'. At one time of course it was an important thoroughfare and acquired the name 'top road' to distinguish it from the valley road, the turnpike road from Keighley to Kendal, along which the important traffic travelled. The Grange is a small hamlet of farms in weathered grey stone and has no medieval buildings, although many of its farms are attractive.

The village, though it is fair still to describe it as rural, has not been untouched by industry. There is a mill, originally a textile mill; the Leeds and Liverpool Canal winds through the village, and now pleasure craft sail on it. In 1847 the Midland Railway between Keighley and Skipton opened, although the station, now demolished, was some distance from the village. The position of the village on the Keighley to Kendal turnpike road meant that considerable traffic passed; in fact traffic has never ceased to whizz round Kildwick Corner. In the early 1820s the Royal Union coach went daily, except Sunday, from Skipton to Leeds, and the Royal Alexander likewise. The mail gig travelled between Bradford and Skipton, and the licensee of the 'White Lion', in the corner opposite the church, was postmaster.

Different is the village of Addingham in the valley of the Wharfe, a place which also abuts onto North Yorkshire; it is a very long village, known as 'Long' Addingham, and it has numerous pubs. The straggling settlement along both sides of a very busy main road is not at first sight inspiring, but there are some interesting old houses along it and also some in the side streets, which has fascinating names such as Stockinger Lane and Druggist Lane. Back from the main road and out of sight of the traffic there is a modern housing development which does not obtrude on the old houses.

Those travellers who came to West Yorkshire in the eighteenth and nineteenth centuries wrote mainly about their travels to the greater centres of population and their impressions of the manufacturing industries, and Wakefield and Leeds figure largely in their writings. But one small village was included by many – the village of Heath. Defoe wrote about it as early as the mid-eighteenth century, but he seemed more impressed with the academy than with the physical aspect of the village, being particularly struck by the proficiency and good order of the pupils – presumably he meant good behaviour. The academy was large enough to house the two hundred young children and had an intimidating array of subjects on offer: natural and experimental philosophy, writing, arithmetic, mensuration, surveying, mechanics, hydrostatics, geometry, trigonometry, astronomy, pneumatics, optics, ethics, metaphysics, drawing, fortification, gunnery, music, dancing etc. A comprehensive range of languages was also offered which included Latin, Greek, French, High Dutch, Low Dutch, Italian, Portuguese and Spanish.

Defoe's eulogy about education concludes with an assessment of the village itself, saying that it was remarkable for a genteel neighbourhood and for healthful air, which was derived from the eminence of the situation.

Housman, at the beginning of the nineteenth century, made a detour on his way to the Lakes in order to see Heath, describing it as a 'village universally allowed to be one of the most beautiful in England',[1] a sentiment which is repeated verbatim

by a later traveller, G. A. Cooke, in an undated work. A guide to
the Wakefield, Pontefract and Goole Railway tells us that Heath
is remarkable 'for the salubrity of its air', while Dibdin remarks
that it is one 'of the sweetest situations and I should suppose
most elegant and sociable neighbourhoods in the kingdom'.[2]

Certainly Heath is no longer sweet, whatever 'sweet' may
mean, unless of course the writer meant that it was sweet in the
sense of not being sour, acrid, smelly and polluted. It is attractive, pleasant, interesting, unique, situated on high ground
above the Calder near an extensive area of common land. In the
sixteenth century Heath Old Hall was built; other wealthy
merchants followed suit, and more houses were built round the
green. Several strands seem to contribute to its uniqueness: it
has preserved its rural aspect although it is so near a large
conurbation; it gives the appearance of an estate village but is
not in fact one.

Heath Hall, as distinct from Heath Old Hall, which is now
demolished, was built by the Smyths, a wealthy family of
woolstaplers who invested surplus capital in landed estate.
John Carr was the architect of Heath Hall, and James Paine the
architect of Heath House, presumably at the same time as he
was building Nostell Priory. In addition to these mansions and
other large houses, there is considerable attractive cottage
property, much of it dating from the seventeenth and eighteenth
centuries.

The village falls naturally into three sections: the northern
area, which is bounded by the park of Heath Old Hall, Heath
House, The Terrace and Cobblers Hall, which housed Heath
Academy in the eighteenth century; the middle area, consisting
of buildings grouped round the 'King's Arms', and the third
area, the group of buildings from Rose Cottage to Heath Farm
and Horse Race End.

It is possible to see in the village the remnants of the pinfold,
the place in which, in the days of the open-field system, stray
animals were shut until they were reclaimed on payment of a
fine by their owners. The old village smithy is still evident, and
the old whittling (gossiping) well.

Cobblers Hall, originally a large house, then academy for
young gentlemen – probably the one which so interested Defoe –

is now three housing units and dates from the early eighteenth century. Other interesting houses are Beech Lawn, a seven-teenth-century house which was at one time occupied by a well-known Quaker family and had associations with John Bright, and the Manor House, which is partly eighteenth and partly nineteenth century and was tenanted in the early twen-tieth century by successive bishops of Wakefield. The King's Arms Inn was probably originally a farmhouse which was converted to an inn in the early nineteenth century, and the King's Arms Cottages have a timber-framed structure of the sixteenth century but were refronted in the eighteenth century.

Ackworth is a large and pleasant village with attractive eighteenth- and nineteenth-century stone buildings. A residen-tial and agricultural village rather than one specializing in a particular trade, its situation between Pontefract and Wakefield meant that it had a great deal of traffic passing through, and it is still very busy. In the early 1820s there was a coach to Scarborough at nine in the morning, to Sheffield at five in the evening, to Lincoln on Mondays, Wednesdays and Fridays at ten in the morning, and to Wakefield Tuesdays, Thursdays and Saturdays at three in the afternoon.

There are buildings in the village which remind us of the coaching age. The 'Boot and Shoe' and the 'Angel' were at one time coaching inns; the former still has a stone mounting-block. There were adequate signposts and directions for travellers; the obelisk in the centre of the village whose shaft dates from before 1700 acted as a guide post. Although it is not now possible to read the inscriptions, the right-hand side facing Bell Lane read 'Wragby, Wakefield', and the left-hand side facing the cross roads read 'Hemsworth, Sheffield'. An early eighteenth century milestone is situated just off the main Wakefield-Doncaster road. The side facing Wakefield is defaced, but the left-hand side reads 'Pontefract three miles', the right-hand side 'Doncaster ten miles' and the back side, facing Ackworth, 'Hessle 1722'. There is another guide post which was erected by the Lords of the Manor in 1805, reading 'Pontefract three miles', 'Hems-worth three miles', 'Snaith fifteen miles', 'Wentbridge three miles' and 'Doncaster three miles'.

Perhaps Ackworth, for those who know it for no other reason, will be familiar for the Friends' School founded here in 1779 and housed in attractive and imposing buildings. There were other schools too in Ackworth, the Mary Lowther School founded in 1741 for 'youths of both sexes' and the Rachel Howard School dating from 1833; the buildings can still be seen. Ackworth was obviously a centre of Nonconformity, as there is a Friends' burial ground and also, very unusually, a burial ground of the Plymouth Brethren.

Not far from Ackworth is the smaller and extremely pleasant village of Wragby, which consists of one short main street lined by small cottages built in a variety of styles, some stone, some stone-faced and some in mellow brick. The war memorial is at the bottom end of the village in front of cottages facing up the street. Surrounded by fields, Wragby is an agricultural village and, not being situated at crossroads, did not have the coaching traffic that Ackworth had; nevertheless traffic passes through it at a great rate. Wragby has one unusual feature: the parish church is not in the village but is situated in the grounds of Nostell Priory.

The villages and hamlets of the uplands high on the hills above the Holme, the Colne, the Calder and the Ryburn were at one time the focal points of the textile industry. Some have developed and been surrounded by urban sprawl so that they merge with the great metropolitan conurbations – Almondbury for example. Others, such as Shelley, Shepley, Sowerby and Kirkburton, are so enlarged that, although it is possible to distinguish the core of the old village, they have become mere suburbs. But while urban absorption is a feature of only some of the villages, common to all of them is their elevation and the resultant steep climb from the valleys to reach them; the lanes and banks from the valleys which were at one time packhorse ways are now metalled. One, at Thurstonland, has a notice saying 'Top of the bank', and just to make sure there is no misunderstanding, at the other side of the road is another saying 'Top o th' Bank'.

Holme is a clustered settlement, described as wild and romantic, right at the head of the Holme Valley with a superb view of it on a clear day and circled by the huge arc of moorland which surrounds it in a great sweep. The fields behind the village give place to rough moorland, and the road snakes over the summit of the hill where the high mast of Holme Moss TV transmitting station dominates the scene. In 1821 Holme had a population of 459; listed were one schoolmaster and twenty-six woollen-manufacturers, and there were two carriers travelling each Tuesday to Huddersfield. There was a thriving industrial community until the middle of the nineteenth century, when Holme began to lose ground to the factories in the valley. Some three-storey weavers' cottages remain as evidence of its former industry; there is a small school which was opened in 1838, and now no longer used as such, a pub, the 'Fleece', several farms and a shop-cum-post office.

The villages of Upperthong and Netherthong had in 1821 populations as follows, Upperthong 1,437, with eight woollen-manufacturers, two grocers and one joiner and cabinet-maker; Netherthong 927, with eighteen woollen-manufacturers, two butchers and three dyers.

The suffix 'thong' is derived from a narrow strip or thong of land, and the prefix 'nether' or 'lower' was attached to distinguish the settlement from the other or upper thong. Netherthong was not a separate settlement at the time of Domesday but formed part of the parish of Meltham. 'Thong' also derived from the Danish word meaning a place of military gathering.

Some of the villagers who lived in Upperthong had donkeys which were used to bring their warps and wefts and to carry the completed piece to market. A system of barter existed between the village farmers and the local grocers and corn-merchants whereby the farmers exchanged their fresh butter for corn. The grain staple among the people in this part of the country was invariably oatmeal, which was stored in 'arkes', or chests, which were frequently valuable items of furniture to be handed down from generation to generation. It was usual for the Upperthong farmers, with either their bare or stockinged feet – some of them kept white stocks specially for the purpose – to tread their oatmeal down into the large chests.

It was customary for the members of the Church of England and the Methodists in the village to hold religious services and meetings in the cottages. In 1836 a public meeting was held, and it was decided to build a school and appoint a master to teach

reading, writing and accounts, and also that the school buildings could be used for the purposes of transacting the public
business of the township. The cost was borne by public subscription, including a house for the master, and the establishment
remained as a day school for about forty years; the building is
still there on the edge of the village, with its inscription giving
the date.

Upperthong is an extremely pleasant village, having one
street called Towngate, which has retained its separate identity
on its windswept height although extensive modern development has taken place and is still taking place lower down the
hillside. The property is well maintained, and there are several
cottages which would have been weavers' cottages in the past.
One of the most attractive corners of the village is a small
courtyard open to the road with cottages round three sides of it.

Netherthong was at one time a centre of Methodism and was
visited by John Wesley, who recorded in his journal for 1772: 'At
ten I preached in the New House at Thong.' A much bigger place
than Upperthong, it has several streets; it is a clustered settlement full of pleasant cottage property, among which are several
one-time weavers' cottages and a pub called the 'Clothiers'
Arms'. Although the old village is intact and largely unspoilt,
there has been modern development on the outskirts.

Thurstonland had a population of 989 in 1821, among them
fifteen woollen-manufacturers, the largest – by a long chalk –
single group of trades, accounting for more than the total
number of other trades listed, and there was also a carrier who
went three times weekly to Huddersfield. The old part of the
village is called simply 'The Village' and contains some well-
built and attractive cottage property, the houses looking much
the same as they must have done at the end of the eighteenth
century except that some have had new windows put in. At one
end of the village is the Methodist chapel and at the other the
Anglican church, while opposite the latter is the school, which
was built in 1766–7 for the education of the poor children of
Thurstonland out of moneys given by the last will of Mrs Ann
Ludlam.

Sowerby stands high on a spur of land overlooking the Ryburn
Valley. From the valley the core of the old village can scarcely

be seen, but the modern urban development, in a variety of building styles, sprawls all over the hillside and reaches the valley. Once in Sowerby, the old village can be seen, with some of the most superb seventeenth-century houses to be found anywhere in the county. In 1821 Sowerby's population was 6,890. Soyland – population in 1821 3,242 – is still an unspoilt hamlet with outlying scattered cottages, modern development having taken place below the old settlement and not peripheral to it as at Sowerby. Soyland had a carrier to Rochdale on Mondays, Wednesdays and Fridays, and to Huddersfield on Tuesdays and Saturdays.

Heptonstall in 1821 had a population of 4,543 but even then was not so important as formerly. In the sixteenth and seventeenth centuries it was a very important place for the production and sale of woollen cloth, so much so that it had its own cloth hall, built by the Waterhouse family of Shibden Hall, Halifax, when they were the lords of the joint manor of Halifax-cum-Heptonstall. The hall was built between 1545 and 1558 and was named Blackwell Hall after the famous cloth market in London, but by the early eighteenth century it had ceased to function as a cloth hall, and clothiers took their wares to the market in Halifax.

There were a great many weavers in the village, and an area where there were many of their cottages has been made into an open space, named Weavers' Square. Silver Street is a row of former handloom weavers' cottages, number 7 being where John Sutcliffe, the last handloom weaver in Heptonstall to practise his craft, lived. (He died in 1902.) A grammar school was endowed in Heptonstall in 1642 and operated as such for about 250 years before closing in 1889. In 1824 the average attendance of the school was between fifty and sixty pupils, who studied English, reading, writing and arithmetic, while seventeen 'free' scholars were taught Latin. The grammar school is now a museum. One of the most unusual features of Heptonstall is its two churches in the same churchyard. The original church was badly damaged in a storm in 1847; it was used until 1854, by which time the new church was complete. Time and the elements effected the deterioration of the fabric so that the internal fittings had to be disposed of. The Methodist church in the

village has an interesting background, being the oldest in
continual use since its inauguration. At one time the Methodist
Sunday School had more than a thousand pupils, seventy-two
teachers, four superintendents and four secretaries. The building is octagonal; apparently John Wesley asked for it to be built
in this way, but difficulty arose when it came to putting on a roof
as nobody knew how to make such a roof. Wesley solved the
problem by having one specially made in Rotherham, and it was
transported across the hills in carts.

Wesley himself visited Heptonstall in 1772, writing in his
journal: 'I preached at Heptonstall to some thousands of people
who stood just before the preaching house on a lovely green
which rises, slope by slope like artificial terraces.'

The 1822 directory has an entry for a place called Queen's
Head, indicating among the most important householders two
grocers, two worsted-manufacturers and three victuallers, one
of the 'Marquis of Granby' and the others, jointly, of the 'Queen's
Head'. Queen's Head, which developed into the present Queensbury, is an example of a textile community establishing itself
high on the hills rather than moving down to the valley. The
naming of the village passed through three stages. It was
originally Causewayend, which probably meant that the village
street was a wild moorland track beyond the reach of the
highway surveyor – even so it was on the main high road from
Hull to Liverpool. Queen's Head was the name used after
Causewayend, but, after a public meeting held on 8 May 1863, it
was decided, by common consent, to call its Queensbury.
Queensbury lies at an altitude of 1,150 feet above sea level, and
it was common in the days of the old Leeds–Rochdale coach to be
asked to 'get out and push' between Bradford and Queensbury,
where there is an ascent of nearly 900 feet. The frequent bus
service from Bradford to Halifax carries no such hazard and,
particularly from the bus's top deck, one can have glorious
views. From Mountain, a summit near Queensbury, it is said
that on a clear day one can see Ingleborough and Penyghent and
also the towers of York Minster.

The reasons for the growth of the community are interlinked:
personality, perseverance and natural resources.

John Foster was born in January 1798, the son of a farmer and colliery-owner, and received his early education at Thornton Grammar School in Bradford. He left this school before he had completed his formal education and worked for a time in business, taking up his schooling at some later date at Brookhouse School, near Ovenden, where he met Jonathan Akroyd. After leaving Brookhouse School he set himself to learn the technicalities of worsted manufacture. In 1819, when he came of age, he established a worsted business of his own at Low Fold, near Queensbury, and soon after married the daughter of Abram Briggs – the family of Briggs was one of the worsted-manufacturers listed in the Directory of 1822. The worsted industry at this time was just beginning to show signs of growth, and in hundreds of cottages in and around Queensbury people were weaving for him. He found a ready market in Bradford and Halifax for the lastings, a hardy, stout and sturdy cloth, and the damask which the firm produced. In 1827 he built a big house, Prospect House, to live in.

By 1832 his business had expanded and he looked for new quarters, eventually taking the tenancy of Cannon Mill, a large factory at Great Horton, and by 1835 he felt able to invest in premises of his own. A farmstead at Black Dyke had been in his wife's family since 1779, and it was on this site that, in 1835, Foster built his mill, superintending the work himself so that the factory was built according to his plans. He went from strength to strength; soon there were three to four thousand spindles at work there; in 1836 power looms were introduced into the Black Dyke Works, and by 1837 Foster was experimenting with alpaca wool.

The Albert Fountain which stands at the entrance to Black Dyke Mills is a work of art in the style of the thirteenth century and was erected by Fosters in memory of the Prince Consort. It was unveiled in May 1863.

In 1876 it was stated that the firm paid £100,000 a year in wages and consumed 15,000 tons of coal and 15,000 packs of alpaca, mohair, English and other wools.

Geographically Queensbury was at a great disadvantage. To reach it by any route meant a very steep climb, and because of its height there was no canal and no railway; it was only the presence of upland coal which enabled the mills to function with

steam power. Any other goods had to rely for transport on
wagons climbing the steep hill; if nothing needed transporting,
one walked: it was not uncommon for a partner in the firm to do a
business journey from Queensbury to Leeds and back on foot, a
distance of thirty miles.

William Foster, John's son, joined the firm in 1842. He was
keenly interested in railways and was chairman of the Bradford
to Thornton Railway, one of whose objects was to get a line
opened to Queensbury. In the early 1870s moves were made for a
rail link between Huddersfield, Halifax and Keighley. After
offering support, the Midland withdrew and the promoters
offered the option to the Great Northern, who were not interested in a line from Huddersfield to Halifax but promised to
extend the Halifax and Ovenden Junction Railway to join the
Bradford and Thornton at Queensbury and continue the lines to
Keighley.

Work on boring the Queensbury tunnel began in May 1874
and was not finished until the end of July 1878; until 1910, when
a longer tunnel near Hertford was opened, Queensbury's was
the longest anywhere on the Great Northern Line. Four streets
of temporary houses were built there to accommodate the
navvies who worked on the line – so temporary that they were
not condemned until 1957.

The railways at Queensbury were unique. The Bradford to
Holmfield section had nearly half its mileage in a tunnel, the
route being named 'the Alpine route' as it was so steep; Queensbury station was the only one in Britain, apart from Ambergate,
which had continuous platforms on three sides of a triangular
junction. There was a steep descent to the station from the town,
and for many years nothing much was done to make the way
pleasant to walk on. One reached the station along 'wretched
footpaths with only one solitary lamp'.[3] Eventually the railway
company did provide a road and built a new and better station.

Queensbury is a bleak, windswept village with houses on both
sides of a long main street, and its height means that, if there is
any snow about, Queensbury will get it. An old history tells that
old-fashioned winters were common there, when the snows that
fell not in frequently levelled up hedge, dyke and road. 'I
wouldn't live there, not if you paid my rates and let me live rent

free,' a woman was heard to remark on the bus. But then, 'Everyone is stalwart and strong at Queensbury; it is not a place for weaklings.'

The Black Dyke Mills are still there and still working, but whereas perhaps not one in a hundred, or even one in a thousand, outside the bounds of Queensbury, would know what they manufacture, probably not one in a hundred has not heard of the Black Dyke Mills Band. John Foster, the founder of the textile firm, played the French horn in the Queenshead Village Band. It was a brass and reed band but in 1855 Foster took over and made it an all brass combination. A band room, new instruments and uniforms were provided; the conductor was Samuel Longbottom, a local musician, and nineteen members of the band worked in the mill of John Foster & Son Ltd. Now, of the twenty-seven regular playing members, only a few are employed in the works, although the firm gives its generous support to the band.

Nineteenth-century housing was pretty poor both for the factory workers and for their country cousins, although the latter had fresh air to mitigate their squalor. There were attempts by some far-sighted factory-owners to build model dwellings for the workers. One of the West Yorkshire model villages was at Copley, near Halifax. Copley Mill was bought by the Akroyd firm in 1844 and, as it was in rather an isolated position, it was decided to build, adjacent to it, dwellings for the workers. There was no doubt that there was the desire to have the workers on the spot for work, but the firm also wished to improve their social and living conditions.

The houses were back to back, some having one bedroom and some two; they cost £90–£120 to build and were rented out at between £4 and £5. 15s. per year. The back-to-back plan of the houses was criticized as a most pernicious principle of house-building. Much more than housing was provided for the workers: a canteen was established in the mill where tea, coffee and soup costing ½d. could be obtained in pint mugs and where meals costing 1½d. or 2d. could be bought. There were allotments in front of the cottages and also a recreation ground. From 1850 a library was provided, and there was a cricket club and a horticultural society; evening classes were started and a

branch of the penny bank opened. A church, St Stephen's, was
also built.

The mill is now demolished, although the houses still exist.
They have a pleasing uniformity and are simple in style, built in
the Gothic idiom so beloved of the Victorians. New houses have
been built on the site of the mill, and the village seems physically to be in two parts, neither bearing any relation to each
other. The church, Anglican, is ornate in style.

The biggest and perhaps the best known of the model villages
is Saltaire, which was built between 1851 and 1871. The street
names are interesting: the main village thoroughfare, as distinct from the through road to Leeds which cuts the village in
two, is called Victoria Road, while a parallel road marking one
limit of the village is Albert Road. The road marking the eastern
limit of the village is Exhibition Road, not without significance.
Other streets are named after members of the Salt family, Titus
Street and Caroline Street (after Mrs Salt).

Titus Salt had made enquiries among his workpeople about
the type of houses they wanted and a number of different types
were built. The majority were two-storey houses with two
bedrooms, a living-room, a working kitchen and a cellar pantry,
the houses costing about £120 each to build. A smaller number
having three bedrooms were built, each with its own garden;
these were most costly, £220 each. In Albert Road larger houses
still were put up for men of the rank of manager. There were also
almshouses in which provision was made for sixty residents,
each single inmate having a pension of 7s. 6d. a week, while
married couples living together each had 5s. a week.

A pamphlet published in 1895 tells that there were 850
cottages varying in rental, as they also varied in size, from 2s.
6d. to 7s. 6d. per week. Every effort had been made to provide
every convenience needed for health and comfort. The streets
were of good width and paved with stone, while the drainage
was constructed on the best sanitary principle. The village had
forty shops but no public house; there was a park for the physical
recreation of villages and an institute with a large reading-room
and a library containing 8,500 volumes. A visitor there during
the 1870s thought that the club and institute building was the
chief architectural triumph of the town. He was also impressed

by the four sculptured lions which were originally intended for the Nelson Monument in London. Two fronted the institute and two the schools, and their names were Vigilance, Determination, War and Peace.

The fees for membership of the institute were arranged to meet the pockets of the workers. During the winter months there were scientific lectures, high class concerts and other attractions. A hospital was built in the village, and there was a church, costing £15,000 and able to seat six hundred. It stands in a large enclosed space between the railway and the canal, surrounded by beautiful lawns and trees and shrubs, and has been described as the most exquisite example of Italian architecture in the kingdom. Its dome seems to dominate the village, and when the light comes from a certain direction, it gleams white.

In 1873 there was the celebration of the twentieth anniversary of the opening of the factory. The people of Saltaire were taken to Bradford on three special trains, accompanied by the Saltaire Brass Band and Rifle Corps. On arriving at the Midland (Forster Square) Station, they formed a procession, four deep, which marched along Market Street and Bridge Street to the Lancashire and Yorkshire Station (Exchange), preceded by the band. There they got into four trains which took them to Lightcliffe, where they were met by the Meltham Mills Band and proceeded towards Crow Nest. There were altogether three bands, Saltaire, Meltham Mills Brass Band and the Black Dyke Mills Band. Entertainment was provided; there was a Punch and Judy Show and an exhibition of athletic sports. One of the workpeople gave a short address which alluded to the two celebrations, the twentieth anniversary of the opening of the works and the seventieth anniversary of the birthday of Sir Titus Salt.

Catering for this large gathering – there were 4,200 guests – was a huge undertaking, involving a vast amount of crockery and victuals. A great tent was erected in the shape of a letter T, each stroke of the T 112 yards long and 16 yards wide. Five rows of tables were erected totalling 1,188 yards in length, the seating being double that length, 2,376 yards, nearly a mile and a half. White glazed calico was used for tablecloths. The weight of crockery and glass was about 11 tons, and it included 10,500 plates, 4,430 china cups and saucers, 1,050 glass 'salts and mustards', 400 large meat dishes, 200 large jugs, 360 pint milk-jugs, 360 slop-basins, 360 sugar-basins, 500 pickle-dishes.

There were 2,400 pounds of beef and also a baron of beef weighing 195 pounds, 2,146 pounds of ham, 500 pounds of tongue, 896 pounds of sugar, 60 gallons of milk, 125 stones of plain bread, 700 pounds of currant bread, 500 pounds of seed bread, 4,500 tarts, 4,500 plain buns, 140 pork pies, 80 pounds of sponge loaves, about 200 pounds of biscuits, 4,000 currant buns, 3,000 seed buns and 100 stones of apples. In addition to all this, 140 pounds of tea and 300 pounds of butter were provided. The feasters all sang grace before they fell to, and while they ate, bands played.

9

Great Houses

When our medieval forebears built their houses, English oak was plentiful, and it was this which they used for the frames of the buildings, for the beams and joists, for the doors and the panelling. They roofed the buildings with stone slates an inch or more thick, of irregular widths, and fixed them together with oak pegs or pins to oak laths. The window openings were broad and low and were divided into many narrow lights, each of six to nine inches with moulded oak mullions. Plasterwork, often decorated in distemper colouring, on which was frequently painted floral designs in thick black outline, was used to cover the inside walls; plaster ceilings appeared later, about the middle of the sixteenth century. In time the plasterwork on the walls gave place to panelling, and the doors corresponded with the panelling, the outer doors being about three inches thick. Eventually the supplies of oak began to run out, and since stone had become more workable, it was used almost entirely for outside walls.

From the time of Elizabeth I, the houses in West Yorkshire were built of stone and occasionally a combination of stone and brick, hard Millstone Grit being the material most frequently used. House plans did not alter much between the Middle Ages and the end of the seventeenth century. There was one large hall, a general living-room called the 'housebody', of a suitable size to keep it proportionate with the rest of the building and usually facing south or east. Was this term 'housebody', one wonders, the origin of the custom, common in working-class districts in West Yorkshire, of speaking of the living-room as 'the house', distinguishing it in a through house from the front room, known as 'the room' – nothing so pretentious as a parlour?

There were many variations between one house and another, but the typical housebody of the West Yorkshire home was two storeys high and had a large window of many lights in the front and a great open fireplace opposite or at one side, with a stone arched opening. The housebody was generally a lofty apartment open to the roof and had a gallery round three sides, giving access to the bedrooms.

In the bigger houses there was a passage called the 'screens' between the two outer doors, separated by a screen or partition from the actual hall, while in addition to the housebody there was also a parlour and kitchen. The proportions of the houses were nearly always low and broad, and often there were stone gables, usually finished with moulded coping stones.

Houses built before 1500 adhered to the Gothic style of architecture, but in the sixteenth and seventeenth centuries windows divided by mullions into three or more lights were the rule, while eight- or ten-light windows were common. The width of each light was about twelve inches, and a wider or thicker mullion was place at every third or fourth light.

An attractive and curious feature characteristic of the windows of the old Yorkshire houses is the Catherine-wheel or rose window over the porch doorway. These are distinctive to West Yorkshire (in fact, to the old West Riding), are Gothic in form if not in detail and can be seen at East Riddlesden Hall and at Kershaw House, Luddenden. The reason for these windows is not clear; it has been suggested that they had an ecclesiastical design because the small rooms which they lighted were used as private oratories or prayer closets. This has never been proved – or disproved – and it may be that they were merely decorative features.

There are many houses of the traditional type particularly in the Halifax parish, Brearley House, Kershaw House, Clay House, Ovenden Hall, Holdsworth House, Todmorden Hall, to name a few. Gawthorpe Hall, Bingley, and the Paper Hall, Bradford, are others. Some other halls have fallen into decay or have been dismantled and shipped to America. They are extremely attractive buildings, the names of their owners enshrined in the title deeds and conveyances, their histories no more eventful than the minutiae of the daily round, the common

Oakwell Hall, Birstall, an Elizabethan mansion, lying in an oasis of peace very near the M62

Nostell Priory near Wakefield, famous for Chippendale furniture

The Holme Valley from Holme

Hebden Bridge

Sowerby Bridge and the Ryburn Valley—many West Yorkshire
industrial towns are clustered in the valleys near to beautiful
countryside

Shibden Dale: a magnificent valley, broad and U-shaped

Stoodley Pike: the 'stone man',
a monument to peace, is a landmark

Looking towards Halifax from the hillside below Stoodley Pike

Holme—enclosed by a huge arc of moorland

Moorland at Shipley Glen—where 'Bruddersford' men could 'feel the old rocks warming in the sun'

The tramway to Shipley Glen in spring sunshine. It still delights children of all ages

The Keighley and Worth Valley train steams into Damens station on its way to Haworth and Oxenhope

Lumb Bridge, a packhorse bridge in Crimsworth Dean

The Leeds and Liverpool Canal between Silsden and Kildwick

The five rise locks at Bingley have become a big tourist attraction.
They deal with a large number of pleasure craft

Sunday morning sailing at Wintersett reservoir, near Wakefield

task. Some of these houses were, at one time, inhabited by the richer clothiers, but now, too big to be maintained by private families, many have been taken over for other purposes. Todmorden Hall, Kershaw House and Holdsworth House are restaurants-cum-country clubs; Ovenden Hall is a home for elderly residents; Clay House is used by Calderdale Metropolitan Council for administrative purposes, and the Paper Hall in Bradford is in process of being restored.

Although no common origin unites the great houses of the county, certain strands link some of them; the houses of the well-heeled middle class, the wealthy clothiers or less gentry, such as Kildwick, Oakwell and East Riddlesden, represent the best in vernacular architecture. In a different league are the houses of the wealthy families, such as Nostell and Harewood, which were designed by architects and furnished by craftsmen who were destined to become famous. Only two of the houses are linked by ghostly legends. In very many cases posterity has benefited from the generosity and public-spiritedness of those who have saved the buildings from closure or demolition and presented them to public bodies.

A more common strand is the quality of the gardens and grounds. Some are superb: Bramham, for example, of which Bogg, in his 1904 book on the area, wrote: 'The tall trees, beeches mostly, forming the magnificent avenues are amongst the highest in this country; and the delightful spots in the park are too numerous to mention fully'.[1]

Temple Newsam has a thousand acres of ground including gardens, a lake, woodland and parkland. Particularly beautiful at the appropriate times of the year are the rose garden and the colourful displays of azaleas and rhododendrons. Woodland, through which there is a nature trail, forms an attractive part of the scenery. Nostell Priory too has extensive grounds and gardens, but the superb large lake with the pleasant walks round it is the most attractive feature of the grounds. Shibden Park is rather different, being in the nature of a public park. The house stands on an eminence, and the land dips down to the valley with long grassy slopes and, in the bottom, a boating lake and swings, see-saws and a paddling-pool. Harewood House has very attractive grounds including a bird garden.

The spacious grounds of the bigger houses are ideal for special events, and it is for this purpose that some of them are used. The first Leeds Folk Festival was held at Temple Newsam in 1982, while an annual late Summer Bank Holiday event is the very popular Bramham Steam Fair, and Nostell plays host to pop concerts from time to time.

Oakwell Hall, near Birstall, is an attractive Elizabethan mansion with an interesting history. It is situated half a mile or so back from the busy main Bradford to Batley road; a line of pylons crosses the country, and one of them towers above the hall, while the M62 runs just behind it. Even though the hall is surrounded by all the bustle of twentieth-century transport and there are modern houses very near, it is surprisingly rural and pastoral and one feels an atmosphere of tranquillity there. The hall is now administered by Kirklees Metropolitan Council, having been saved more than half a century ago from demolition and transportation to America. Two Harrogate businessmen, Sir Norman Rae and Mr John E. Sharman, in 1928 bought Oakwell Hall and handed it over to Birstall Urban District Council. In 1937 Birstall was absorbed into Batley, and matters concerning Oakwell Hall were managed by a committee consisting of six members of Batley Town Council and a representative from each of three learned societies, the Thoresby Society, the Yorkshire Archaeological Society and the Brontë Society. For of course Oakwell Hall has important connections with the Brontës as it was here that Charlotte set her novel *Shirley*, using not the name Oakwell but that of Fieldhead, nearby, where Joseph Priestley was born.

The manor of Oakwell was within the manor of Gomersal but was probably not known by its own name in the early Middle Ages as no document has been found bearing the name before the early fourteenth century. A document of 1311 exists stating that John de Tilly was the lord of Okewell. His forebears had been Lords of Gomersal for almost two hundred years, the manor being granted to the family by the de Lacis.

Oakwell remained in the hands of the Tilly family for some 450 years and about the year 1570 came into the hands of Henry Batt of Haley Hill, Halifax. Henry had a son named John who, in 1583, built the present Oakwell Hall. It is strange to visualize these stately buildings in the course of construction; because they have been there for as long as one can remember, one, albeit unconsciously, thinks of them as part of the landscape. But Oakwell Hall would be new at a time when affairs of state were weighty, when the air was heavy with intrigue as the Roman Catholics plotted to overthrow Elizabeth I and put Mary, Queen of Scots, on the throne, when Drake and Hawkins were raiding King Philip's treasure ships and when, in 1588, the Armada was defeated. News travelled slowly in those days, and it would be the state and progress of the new buildings which would engage the minds and tongues of the villagers rather than the prospect of a Spanish Armada.

The hall is built of local dressed stone and roofed with local grey stone slates. At the front there are large ten-light mullioned windows and a low Tudor porch over which is carved in stone the initials of John Batt with the date 1583, while inside the porch are stone seats which would provide a shady retreat from the heat of summer, and the door is of heavy oak. Inside the house the vestibule and passage have fine plasterwork on the ceiling, consisting of octagons connected by hexagons and pentagons with irregular sides.

Turning left from the passage, one enters the Great Hall with its screen of three pairs of classical columns, its great open fireplace and spacious mullioned windows. From the Great Hall is the withdrawing-room referred to in an early seventeenth-century inventory as 'the Great Parlour', there being also a little parlour. At the rear of the hall is a window over which the letters DIRY can be seen; this was to indicate a dairy, an important sign, as dairies were exempt from window tax, instituted in 1696 and subject to several amendments before being eventually repealed in 1851. In 1795 dairies were exempted: 'It shall not be lawful to charge any window or lights in any dairies or in any room used for the sole purpose of drying and keeping cheese and butter . . . Owners shall paint on the door thereof in large Roman block letters of two inches at the least in height and of a proportional breadth the words DAIRY or CHEESE ROOM and shall keep such words distinctly legible.' It is sometimes possible to spot the word 'dairy' over small windows in farmhouses. There is an example at a farm on the top road between Kildwick and Silsden; some years ago the word was sharply and clearly chiselled out, but time and weather have taken their toll, and it is now scarcely decipherable, although the D is quite clear. Butter, cream and cheese made in the dairy at Oakwell were sold in Wakefield and also nearer Oakwell.

There is a ghost at Oakwell Hall. In 1684 it was said that the ghost of William Batt appeared on horseback and was seen to approach the Hall, dismount from his horse and enter. Walking to the staircase at the right-hand corner, he climbed the stairs and entered the north-west bedroom where he vanished; at the entrance to this bedroom a bloody footprint was discovered. The mark of it was, at a later date, removed by the then owner and a square of white wood put in to mark the spot. William Batt was killed, according to the Reverend Oliver Heywood, at Barnet near London and was buried at Birstall on 30 December 1684 – the day that the apparition appeared. The register at Birstall church records the burial of William Batt of 30 December 1684 but does not say how he died.

Many miles from Oakwell, high above the Aire Valley and commanding a splendid view of it, stands Kildwick Hall. The village and manor of Kildwick were granted in 1124 by Cecilia de Romillé of Skipton Castle to the religious house at Embsay, which was afterwards removed to Bolton and known as Bolton Priory. For the next four hundred years the estate was managed by the Canons of Bolton, and there was no resident landlord. At the Dissolution of the Monasteries the property at Kildwick eventually came into the hands of Hugh Currer in 1558, and remained with him until he died in 1617. It then passed through five generations of his descendants, named in order, Henry, Hugh, Henry, Haworth and Henry. Some of them, especially Haworth Currer (1690–1744), were active magistrates whose names frequently appear in the records of the West Riding Quarter Sessions. There is a monument in Kildwick Church which says of Haworth Currer: 'he was a great proficient in the study of the Law, but allured by the charm of a private life he retired to the place of his birth, where he choose [sic] rather to employ the talents he had acquired therein to the dispensation of justice on the bench than to the advancement of his own private fortune in attendance at the bar.' Of his son, Henry

Currer, it states: 'after maintaining the reputation of his family, in hospitality and the distribution of justice, he exchanged this life in hopes of a better.'

One wonders if Charlotte Brontë was so impressed by the name Haworth Currer that this induced her to adopt the *nom de plume* Currer Bell.

Dorothy Currer (1687–1763), the last of the family, married Dr Richard Richardson whose family had for two hundred years owned Bierley Hall, Bradford.

Richard Richardson's grandson Henry married Margaret Clive Wilson, the daughter of Mathew Wilson of Eshton Hall and after his death she married her cousin Mathew Wilson. Her daughter by her first marriage, Miss Frances Mary Richardson Currer, owned the estate until 1861 and was succeeded by her half-brother Mr (afterwards Sir) Mathew Wilson, the first MP for the Skipton Division, and he by his grandson Colonel R. H. F. W. Wilson.

The hall is a fine gabled building with well-proportioned windows, those in the two lower floors having transoms as well as mullions. The date of the building is probably 1670; the coat of arms over the front door is that of Hugh Currer (1608–90) and his wife. The kitchen, which has a fine arched fireplace, and the room above it are probably the housebody and chamber of Hugh Currer's manor house. On the west side of the terrace is a room which was used as a billiard room but which was probably first built as a justice room – the Currers were active magistrates, and no doubt this is where Petty Sessions were held.

At the end of the eighteenth century and the beginning of the nineteenth, when the hall was occupied not by the owner but by tenants, many parts of the building were used by hand woolcombers. It is a novel concept that these halls of the wealthy were used by villagers and 'ordinary people' and not just lived in by the well-to-do. The gateway is impressive, being guarded by the Kildwick Lions who, when they hear the church clock strike twelve, go down to the river to drink. Across the road from the gateway was a superb landscaped garden with a fountain and a ball dancing in the play of the water. But time marched on and Kildwick Hall became an hotel. The garden lacked attention and soon assumed an unkempt, neglected and overgrown appearance. Now, however, a different style of landscaping has transformed the tatty decay into an adequate and attractive car-park, enhanced by the presence of many trees.

Further down the Aire Valley in a low-lying position next to the main Bradford–Keighley road is East Riddlesden Hall, a large house which was bought by W. A. Brigg and J. J. Brigg – who in fact lived at Kildwick Hall – and presented by them to the National Trust. From about the middle of the twelfth century until the latter half of the fourteenth, when it became divided into two estates, East and West Riddlesden was held by the Maude family, who also held land in Flintshire. In 1402 one of the daughters of the family married Robert Paslew, who belonged to a family of good standing at Potternewton, near Leeds, and the East Riddlesden estate passed to them. Towards the end of the sixteenth century financial difficulties meant that the family needed to sell some of their land. An Ellen Paslew had married a Robert Rishworth from Coley in Halifax parish, and in 1591 the estate was transferred to Robert Rishworth. But the Rishworths did not reign long, selling the estate in 1638 to James Murgatroyd, a rich clothier from Warley in the parish of Halifax reputed to be worth £2,000 a year.

There was an interesting lawsuit between him and Lady Anne Clifford. Leases had been drafted in the days when it was customary to pay rent partly in money and partly in produce. Lords of manors were accustomed with their servants to travel from one manor to another to receive their rents, and it was useful for them to know that adequate provisions for the men and their horses would be available. It had been customary, continuously over a period of four hundred years, for Skipton Castle to receive each year from tenants – in addition to rent – eight hundred boon hens, and likewise Appleby Castle. Murgatroyd was due to pay one hen. When he was asked for this, he refused. Lady Anne Clifford was as determined to have the hen, which was her right, as he was to avoid payment. To give in to him might have meant subsequently giving in to all the rest of the tenants, resulting in a possible loss of sixteen hundred hens annually. She therefore brought an action against him at York Assizes, which she won, receiving the hen, although it cost her £200. It cost Murgatroyd the same. Unfortunately the picturesque and Gilbertian addition to the story, that Lady Anne invited Murgatroyd to dine, serving up the hen for dinner, is a figment of someone's romantic imagination.

The Murgatroyd family apparently flourished on tangling with the law, as the three sons of James along with a Thomas Bradley and his wife were summoned before the Council of the North accused of divers offences and misdemeanours committed in the chapel yard and porch of Luddenden. Imagination boggles! They were fined the rather odd sum of £67, while their father was fined £500. Additionally they had to do penance and were excommunicated for two years. The Council of the North was a most hated instrument of the tyranny of Charles I, but James Murgatroyd bore no grudge, for on his new building at Riddlesden he carved likenesses of Charles I and his Queen with the legend 'Vive le Roy'. He died in 1653, and through his daughter (the Murgatroyd family fortune had been lost by the sons) the estate passed to the Starkies. Mary Murgatroyd had married Nicholas Starkie, and the family were the last resident owners of the hall.

On the left as one comes through the gate is the fine timbered barn, one of the finest in the north of England, having eight bays with huge oak pillars supporting the arched timbers of the roof. The central floor, like the nave of a church, measures 120 feet by 40 feet, while on each side and at the end are 'aisles' divided into stalls for the cattle.

The battlemented two-storey building on the left is known as the chapel although there seems to be no justification for this. It is on these battlements that there are the likenesses of Charles I and his Queen and the motto. The hall itself is in three sections; the battlemented north porch is a striking feature because it has a Catherine-wheel window, the design of which is unique. The windows of the lower storeys of this part of the hall are double lighted with mullions and transoms. The middle part of the hall is commonly known as the Banqueting Hall and was at one time one of the chief rooms, with an open arched fireplace. The kitchen is a stone-flagged room with a low arched fireplace; on its east side is the dining-room, while on the south side is the drawing-room, both having oak panelling and an ornamental plaster ceiling.

On the outskirts of Halifax stands the one-time house of a yeoman clothier which is now a museum. The house itself, Shibden Hall, has been filled with furniture, implements and so on to give a vivid picture of those who occupied it. In addition to this the outbuildings have been adapted as a folk museum to show the various crafts which were necessarily practised in order to maintain and support life before the age of mass production.

William Otes first built a house on the site towards the beginning of the fifteenth century, but it was altered by the succeeding families who inhabited it; after the Otes family there were the Saviles, the Waterhouses and the Listers. In 1933 John Lister died at the age of 87, being the last of the line which had lived in the hall for 321 years. In 1923 A. S. McCrea had bought the hall from Lister but allowed him to spend the rest of his life there, and on Lister's death McCrea gave the hall to Halifax Corporation. It is now maintained by the Museum Department of Calderdale Metropolitan Council.

The first house known to have been on the site was probably built about 1420 and consisted of the two timbered gables with the centre front. The centre portion, instead of being of stone as it is today, was also timbered and stood about thirty inches behind the present front. The room behind this front, the housebody, was open to the roof, and light was admitted through wooden mullioned windows. In 1590 Robert Waterhouse built the small wing butting onto the back of the housebody. Before then, it is thought, there was an external staircase to a gallery which ran across the back wall of the housebody linking the two gables. The Waterhouse wing consisted of a basement dairy, a room at ground-floor level used as a buttery and one room above. In 1660 the stone front was built and the housebody divided into two rooms by a floor placed approximately at the top of the present panelling. A new wooden mullioned window was built next to the porch window to light a 'flesh chamber' where the salted meat was hung. Anne Lister built the tower and the east wing. She also pulled out the seventeenth-century floor in the housebody, leaving it open to the roof, and she repanelled the room.

Several more large houses have been presented to a local

authority through the generosity of some private benefactor. One, administered now by the Bradford Metropolitan Council, is Bolling Hall which was presented to Bradford Corporation, as it then was, by Mr G. A. Paley.

Dr Whitaker, in his *Loidis and Elmete*, an antiquarian work of 1816 dealing with much of West Yorkshire, said of Bolling Hall: 'The Hall is a large and majestic building with a centre and two deep wings to the north and has been built at different periods.' In fact so many additions and alterations have been made to the building by various owners that it now has a somewhat mixed appearance.

Bolling's most famous claim – apart from the fact that it is now a very interesting museum – is its connection with the Civil War, and there are different versions of the story.

At the time of the Civil War between King and Parliament in the seventeenth century, Bolling Hall was in the hands of the Tempest family. Richard Tempest invited the Earl of Newcastle to make his headquarters at Bolling Hall, and the Earl spent two or three days positioning his cannon, while the townsfolk are said to have converted the parish church into a fortress and hung woolsacks on the tower. Thus prepared to withstand the coming siege, battle commenced, and when it was over, the Parliamentary army under Lord Fairfax was driven out of the town.

An alternative version of the story is somewhat more picturesque. The Earl of Newcastle, having captured the town during the second siege, was greatly exasperated by the stubborn resistance of the inhabitants, many of whom were staunch Parliamentarians. He gave orders that the town was to be sacked and that the inhabitants, every man, woman and child, were to be slaughtered. While he was asleep a female apparition visited him:

> Mournful she seemed, though young and fair
> She clasped her hands as if in prayer
> And, sighing said 'In pity spare
> Our poor devoted town.'[2]

After the visitation of this apparition, the Earl sent out orders revoking his former command, the lives of all the unarmed inhabitants of the town were spared and the place became a garrison for the King. Richard Tempest was fined £1,748 for his part in the Civil War, and this placed him in such financial difficulty that he had to dispose of the manor of Bolling.

Leeds Metropolitan Council is the custodian of two 'stately homes'. One, Lotherton Hall, a nineteenth-century house at Aberford, is a comparatively recent acquisition, having been given to Leeds by Sir Alvary and Lady Gascoigne in 1968.

The Gascoigne family had its origins in Gascony before the Norman Conquest. In the fourteenth century they were settled on estates at Gawthorpe and Harewood; the Parlington Estate, immediately west of Aberford, was acquired in 1546. Sir John Gascoigne, the first baronet, succeeded in 1602, and until the death of the eighth baronet, Sir Thomas Gascoigne, in 1810, there was a continuous succession. Under his will the estates passed to Richard Oliver of County Limerick who assumed the name and arms of Gascoigne and lived at Parlington. The Lotherton half of the estate passed to his grandson, Colonel Frederick R. T. T. Gascoigne in 1893. He succeeded to Parlington in 1905 but sold the contents and continued to live at Lotherton until his death in 1937. It then became the property of Sir Alvary Gascoigne, his son.

The central section of the house probably dates from sometime after 1760. Colonel F. R. T. T. Gascoigne extended the house – alterations which were completed in 1896. There were further extensions in 1908, while in 1903 the house was considerably extended towards the west. The chapel dates from the late twelfth century, but the present entrance was made during the eighteenth century.

Temple Newsam, a large mansion in the east of the city, is also administered by Leeds Metropolitan Council. The two first recorded owners of the Temple Newsam estate were two Anglo-Saxons, the Thanes Dunstan and Glunier, but at the time of Domesday it was part of the Honour of Pontefract.

In 1155 Henry de Laci confirmed the handing-over of the manor to the Knights Templars in exchange for lands in Nottinghamshire. The Order of Knights Templars had been conceived by a Burgundian knight about the year 1119 as a means of safeguarding pilgrims to the Holy City from the raiding Saracens. They acquired land all over Europe and had numerous gifts of land in England. The Order eventually sank into disrepute and, at the beginning of the fourteenth century, Edward II ordered the arrest of all Knights Templars. Temple Newsam had been efficiently farmed by them, and it was a valuable estate. In spite of the Pope's wish that the property of the Knights Templars should be transferred to the Order of Knights Hospitallers, Edward II seized Temple Newsam, and the next few years seem to have been a sort of Box and Cox between the Knights Hospitallers and the Crown. The Knights Hospitallers seized the manor for a short time in 1323 and were eventually allowed to retain the church at Whitkirk and the Templars' manor courts of Whitkirk and Leeds Kirkgate-cum-Holbeck. In 1314 Edward II had granted the manor to Sir Robert Holland, a soldier of fortune who held it until 1323 when he was deprived of his estates for having taken part in a campaign against the King's favourite. The manor was therefore tenantless, and it was then seized by the Knights Hospitallers. Edward forced them to quit and the manor was restored to the Crown.

The manor at some subsequent time was given to the widow of the Earl of Pembroke, the founder of Pembroke College, Cambridge, and then to the Darcy family and subsequently reverted to the Crown again. When Elizabeth I came to the throne, Temple Newsam became a centre of Catholic intrigue for the staunch Roman Catholics who regarded Mary, Queen of Scots, as the rightful occupant of the throne and aimed to depose Elizabeth. The estates of Temple Newsam were therefore confiscated from their then owners, the Lennox Stuarts, and managed by a resident agent.

In 1603, when James I came to the English throne, he granted Temple Newsam to Ludovick, Duke of Lennox, but the Duke was constantly in debt and in 1622 he found it necessary to sell his estate. The purchaser was Sir Arthur Ingram, and the estate was in the hands of this family for a long time.

In 1661 the second grandson of the first Arthur Ingram was made a peer of Scotland with the style Baron Ingram and Viscount Irvine (his family used the English form Irwin). The ninth Viscount died in 1778, leaving a widow and five daughters. The widow was succeeded in 1807 by her eldest daughter Isabella, Marchioness of Hertford. She died in 1834 and was succeeded by her sister who died in 1841. Her younger sister, the third of the five daughters of the ninth Viscount, had married Hugo Meynell. Their son Hugo Charles Meynell succeeded to the estate, taking the name Meynell Ingram. In 1869 he was followed by his son Hugo Francis, who died two years later, leaving the estate to his widow. On her death in 1904 the estate passed to her nephew, the Hon. Edward Wood. In 1922, for the first time in three centuries, Temple Newsam changed hands by purchase, bought by Leeds City Council.

The house is a symmetrical arrangement of three wings under a single roof. The earliest part dates from the time of Thomas, Lord Darcy, who built a large square house with a central courtyard, probably before 1521. Soon after Sir Arthur Ingram got the house, he proceeded to modernize it. By pulling down the east wing and reconstructing the north and south wings, he made a typical E plan. He built the grand porch which bears the Ingram coat of arms and placed a loyal and pious inscription round the balustrade: 'All Glory And Praise Be Given To God The Father The Son And Holy Ghost On High Peace On Earth Goodwill Towards Men Honour And True Allegiance To Our Gracious King Loving Affection Amongst His Subject Health And Plenty Be Within This House.'

In 1674 the old roof on the west wing was renewed. During the second half of the eighteenth century John Carr, 'Capability' Brown and the Brothers Adam were consulted about rebuilding the south wing, and in 1796 the widow of the ninth Viscount remodelled it. Towards the end of the nineteenth century Mrs Meynell Ingram replaced most of the Georgian sash windows with stone mullions and leaded lights and rebuilt the north porch, placing her coat of arms over the doorway.

A nineteenth-century visitor was not really impressed with his visit to Temple Newsam. He commented on the balustrade: 'This edifice has a great singularity, instead of battlements, a stone gallery surrounds the roof consisting of letters which compose a sentence from the Bible.'[3] He went on to say that the park was melancholy and the furniture of the house old-fashioned without being interesting.

Although most of the 'stately' homes in West Yorkshire have been bought and presented to the National Trust or to the local authority or turned into hotels, some are still family homes.

One is Bramham Park, which was built by the first Lord Bingley in 1698. His father, Robert Benson, came from Wrenthorpe, near Wakefield, and had twice been Lord Mayor of York and five times MP for the city. He had enclosed land at Bramham Moor. The younger Benson, a man of great ability and culture, was also Lord Mayor of York and MP for the city. He was a favourite of Queen Anne – tradition has it that she stayed at Bramham – and in 1713 was created Lord Bingley. He later went to Spain as ambassador. When travelling abroad he saw some gardens designed by Le Nôtre, and it was these which gave him inspiration. The T canal, the Obelisk pond and the cascades at Bramham are suggestions of Le Nôtre, but, in fact, he never came to England.

There is also uncertainty about the architect of the house, but John Wood, who later became famous for his work at Bath, had a subsidiary hand in it. It was James Paine who designed the chapel in the garden.

Another house still occupied by a private family is Nostell Priory, a name which is rather misleading as the word 'priory' evokes a picture of an ecclesiastical structure. The land was in the gift of Ilbert de Laci, and his son Robert gave it to the Augustinian Order between 1109 and 1114. Their priory was built near the site of a Saxon hermitage and was dedicated to St Oswald. The canons of Nostell worked the coal seams. At some time subsequent to the Dissolution of the Monasteries, Nostell was owned by Sir Thomas Gargrave who was the Speaker of the House of Commons in the time of Queen Elizabeth. In 1613 it was bought by Sir John Wolstenholme, the son of the man who made the sailing of the *Mayflower* possible. In 1654 the estate was bought by Rowland Winn, an alderman of London, who conveyed it to his brother George. The old priory was used as a residence until the present house was built.

In 1733 Rowland Winn commissioned James Paine to build a new house near the old priory, which was subsequently pulled down. Paine was only nineteen years at the time, and this was his first building of any importance. Little might have been heard of him had it not been for Rowland Winn. The façade we see today is the work of Paine, with the exception of the wing which was added later by Robert Adam. Inside a few of Paine's fine rooms remain. The new priory appears to have been completed in 1740, and in 1741 a marriage licence was issued to James Paine and Sarah Jennings of Wragby.

The general layout of lakes, avenues and gardens derives from various designers of whom little is known, Joseph Perfect, Stephen Switzer and a Mr Greening.

In 1765 Sir Rowland Winn died and was succeeded by his son, Sir Rowland the fifth baronet, who did not consider the house big enough and called on Robert Adam to build four new wings and redecorate and furnish the interiors in accordance with his newer manner. Only one wing, however, was erected, but Adam was responsible for the riding-school and part of the stables. The three craftsmen who worked with him were Joseph Rose, Antonio Zucchi and Thomas Chippendale. Most of the plasterwork was completed before 1766 and 1777 at a cost of £1,822. 3s. Nostell is one of the West Yorkshire 'stately homes' which is famous for Chippendale furniture.

At the other end of the county is another 'stately home' which is famous for the furniture of Thomas Chippendale. The present Harewood House is the last of three houses: the first was the castle, which is believed to have been erected by William de Curcy about the middle of the twelfth century. Sometime in the sixteenth century it came into the possession of the Gascoignes of Gawthorp by marriage. Gawthorp was a separate manor in the township of Harewood, and the hall was situated about 350 yards south of the present Harewood House. The last of the Gascoignes to own Harewood was Sir William, Lord Chief Justice of England.

In 1580 the estate passed to the Wentworths, and in 1657 it had to be sold by the son of the ill-fated Earl of Strafford. In 1738 it was bought by Henry Lascelles, whose son Edwin demolished Gawthorp and built the present house of stone from a nearby quarry. The foundations were laid in 1759, and it was completed in 1771. The services of a well-known architect, John Carr, were obtained; in fact Carr was responsible for the whole village of Harewood. His original elevations were modified and slightly

altered by Robert Adam, whom Lascelles engaged to co-operate
with Carr. In 1843 Sir Charles Barry added another storey to
each of the pavilion wings and surrounded the entire roof with
heavy Corinthian balustrades. One of the greatest treasures of
Harewood is the large collection of furniture by Thomas Chippendale. The park and gardens are the work of 'Capability'
Brown.

Two nineteenth-century visitors had differing views of Harewood. One tells us that Harewood House is a magnificent stone
mansion judiciously situated on a hill: 'But nothing within
interests the mind; no productions of the arts, unless indeed the
labours of the gilder and upholster may be considered as deserv-
ing that character. Rich hangings and fine furniture may catch
the gaze and captivate the fancy of the multitude, but taste and
sensibility require some other food and turn away with satiety
from the glitter of golden cornices and the lustre of satin
hangings.' They (the people who visit Harewood) 'will be more
gratified in visiting the little ancient church, uniform and neat,
half embosomed in a clump of trees in the park and containing
six table monuments',[4] which he proceeds to describe at great
length.

Another visitor, nearly thirty years later, was more fulsome
in his praise. He thought Harewood House 'a delightful residence in a superb situation . . . fine natural wood, with glens,
rocks, a copious mountain stream, the ruin of an old castle on a
hill, all situated in the richest country and with distinct views of
the Cumberland mountains'.

Lord Harewood had returned from a hunt, and the visitor was
most impressed with the way the dogs were kept and treated.
His host took him on a tour through the house, '. . . which is
richly and handsomely furnished, and contains family pictures
by Vandyk, Reynolds and Lawrence'. What impressed him was,
'. . . red curtains painted on wood, so admirably executed that
Rauch himself would have been astounded at the flow of the
drapery. Though I was told what they were, I could scarcely
believe it till I convinced myself by the touch, so completely
deceptive was the imitation of the silken stuff.'[5]

King George V's daughter, the Princess Royal, married one of
the Lascelles family and lived at Harewood House.

10

Countryside

When W. H. Scott, a writer at the turn of the century, outlined
the great diversity to be found in the county of Yorkshire, he
was, of course, writing not of West Yorkshire, or even of the
West Riding, but of the old county of Yorkshire, comprising the
East, North and West Ridings. He wrote:

> There is one Yorkshire of Sheffield and another of Teeside. There is
> the Yorkshire of Bradford and Halifax, of Huddersfield and the Spen
> Valley, and of Wakefield and Pontefract and the colliery districts.
> There is the Yorkshire of the Dales and the Wolds, of the great
> Cleveland iron-stone country and the long line of coast from Humber
> to Tees, of the solitary moorlands in the north-west, and there is the
> Yorkshire of the low-lying country about Thorne and Goole and
> Howden. Wherever you go in this county as big as a kingdom you will
> find diversity.
>
> Go westward from Leeds and you traverse for the most part a series
> of treeless valleys overrun by blackened stone walls and gaunt mill
> chimneys. Go to the south-west and there are pit shafts marring the
> would-be charms of the landscape. Go in a north-westerly direction
> and you are again confronted by factory buildings. Only as the River
> Aire narrows to a tiny stream does the prospect improve. But, make
> your exit on the northern or on the eastern side and you need not
> travel five miles to enjoy rural delights.[1]

These rural delights are now, of course, in North Yorkshire.

The reconstituted county can be likened to a wedge of cheese,
with the high ground lying to the west, gradually sloping to the
eastern plain, and there is still contrast: one of the most attractive and noticeable features of the county is its diversity.

Although the area is heavily industrialized and urbanized, there is still a considerable amount of farming, and this too shows contrast. Sheep are reared on the uplands, while in the Pennine valleys, the Aire, the Wharfe, Holme, Colne and Calder, there are small dairy farms which in most cases are worked by owner-occupiers, the farmers having grass crops for hay and silage but usually no sheep. There are small farms on the outskirts of the towns and in rural pockets between the large conurbations, while away from the Pennine highlands the pattern of land-ownership is different; here are big estates, and the agricultural pattern changes to arable and livestock farming. To the north and east of Leeds, stretching from Adel-cum-Eccup as far as Wetherby and Thorp Arch, the area is predominantly rural and the farming mainly arable, although there are some large dairy herds. In the southern part of the county, where the textile manufacturing industry gives way to mining, between and around the colliery villages there is rich agricultural land which coincides with an area of large estates. The type of farming here is mixed, with cereal, cash roots, pigs, poultry and dairying being the main enterprises.

Building-materials change too, from the sandy-coloured stone and red-tiled roofs in the north-east of the county, through the harsher Millstone Grit of the Pennine industrial area, with stone houses and slate roofs, to the red brick of the southern part of the county. In the Millstone Grit area, where stone was plentiful, the fields are enclosed by stone walls, whereas to the north and south hedges and fences predominate.

Scott's remarks about the series of treeless valleys is patently not true, for the wealth of trees in small and large clusters which fill the valley floors and flourish on the hillsides is one of the finest features of West Yorkshire's valleys. The mills and chimneys, rather than disfiguring the landscape, add a certain dignity to it; similarly the pit shafts which he claims mar the scene have a geometric precision which is not unpleasing. It is not the mills, the chimneys, the rows of millworkers' and colliers' cottages, the mine shafts and the slag heaps, legacies of the Industrial Revolution, which disfigures the landscape but the twentieth-century tat. The regularity and uniformity of nineteenth-century building is neither ugly nor displeasing.

But the hotch-potch of different building styles, the vast housing estates creeping higher up the hillsides and eating up the
countryside, the sheds, garages and mills in a multiplicity of
styles and variety of building-materials which clutter the valleys – herein lie the squalor and disfigurement.

Our Anglo-Saxon and Viking forebears have left, along with
more tangible evidence of their occupation of the north,
considerable rich additions to the language. All six northern
counties use the word 'dale' for 'valley', although perhaps the
Yorkshire Dales are the most famous. In West Yorkshire is part
of two of them, Airedale and Wharfedale, and the whole of
another, Calderdale. The word 'Calderdale' is significantly new,
coming into common use after local government reorganization.
It is interesting that the valleys of the Holme and the Colne are
not called dales but 'the Holme valley' and 'the Colne valley'.
There are smaller dales which are of great beauty, and many of
them of great interest.

One of these is Cragg Vale. From the Lancashire border the
road descends gradually to Mytholmroyd, flanked on either side
by broad expanses of open moorland with rough grazing and, as
the valley becomes narrower and the hills steeper, there is an
abundance of pasture land with thick woods in the valley
bottom. These steep-sided hills are rugged and scarred with
rocks and pitted with tiny valleys – the place-names Cragg,
Whams and Clough reflect this. The old name for the stream was
Turvin Brook, the place where turf was cut, while the name
Rud, where red ochre for staining sheep was obtained, occurs in
a side valley.

At the head of Cragg Vale – it is interesting that the name
embraces not only the valley but also the settlement – there is a
tributary valley having mixed woodland with a preponderance
of silver birch. At either side the hills rise smoothly, and by the
side of the stream a road snakes into the hills across the
moorland and down into Mankinholes, for this was, at one time,
a packhorse track. As far as the high moorland the road is
metalled, but once on the moor it gives place to the characteristic flagstones of the packhorse way. At the bottom of the valley a
mill chimney remains as evidence of early industry, and a
strategically placed inn is a welcome source of refreshment for

travellers. Where the valley widens stands the church, a neat, although quite modern building, dating from 1839. From it, the road, Church Bank, climbs steeply to the main valley.

Perched on the hillsides are the old farms, while more modern settlements are the rows of cottages lying parallel to the main road. Those at the top of Church Bank are four storeys high on the lower side and two storeys at the main valley, or upper, side, a characteristic form of building in the steep valleys. It is a busy dale with a lot of through traffic, and a sign on a group of three- and four-storey houses, Four Gates End, indicates the considerable traffic of former times. A caravan park at its lower end is well patronized, for of course this is an ideal spot to spend a holiday, as there is excellent walking country, it is a peaceful rural area and, for those who wish to travel, an excellent centre for visiting places of interest further afield.

Physically the rough terrain, the rocky outcrops, the tiny hollows and dells, which scar and pit the hillsides, are ideal ingredients for adventure – common a couple of hundred years ago when the valley was a centre for the illegal activities of coiners.

Beating the system will always have a fascination for a certain type of person. Smugglers and coiners were the old equivalent of those who try to evade income tax and defraud social security. Partly perhaps because smugglers and coiners dealt in goods rather than juggled figures on paper, and also because distance lends enchantment, the present has endowed these nefarious activities with a certain romance and excitement.

Coining, 'the yellow trade' as it has been called, was not indigenous to Yorkshire but came from Birmingham. In the middle of the eighteenth century David Hartley was travelling in the Midland area where he was introduced to coining and on coming back to his native land he told some of his friends about it. As the tools which were required were neither sophisticated nor expensive – a good pair of scissors and a sharp knife – it is not surprising that the information and practice spread and that some made a living out of coining.

With the scissors the coiner deftly clipped the rim from the coin; with the file, he milled the edge. The clippings were put into an iron pot on the fire to be melted and then put into a brass mould where they were hammered out to the correct dimensions. After this they received the impression from a pair of stamps, small square pieces of steel fitting together with the obverse and reverse of the coins engraved on them. The coins most generally counterfeited were guineas and half and quarter guineas, although some of the coiners went in for coins of smaller denomination such as shillings and halfpennies. But of course they had to have coins in the first place, and these were supplied by merchants and manufacturers who made a profit from the increased number of coins they possessed. It is true the forged coins were smaller, but they were passable.

So great the fraud that eventually the Mint sent an officer named Deighton to bring the evil-doers to justice. Taking up his headquarters in Halifax, he realized that the villains he had to deal with were desperate men. However, using bribery, he not only managed to get the men talking but also caused dissension among them. In this way 'King David' was committed to York Castle on the information of a man named Broadbent which was given under the promise of a gift of 100 guineas. Broadbent repented of his treachery to the coiners and went to York twice, declaring that the information he had given was false. He tried to get the release of 'King David' but he was too late, and Hartley was executed in 1769.

At the same time as Broadbent was seeking to undo the consequences of his action, Hartley's brother murdered Deighton, who, by means of a forged letter, was delayed on his way home until late at night when he was waylaid and shot in a narrow alley. The reward of the murderers was 100 guineas, which was collected by fellow coiners, who also provided a celebration supper. In turn a reward of £200 was offered for *their* capture. Eventually they were taken and hanged on Beacon Hill, their bodies a macabre warning to other incipient wrongdoers.

The extent of unity among the coiners and the lengths to which they were prepared to go was apparent in the village of Heptonstall two years after the execution of 'King David'. In 1771 a man offered to give evidence about the murderers of Deighton was set upon by a gang of coiners who thrust his head into the fire, placed a pair of red-hot tongs round his neck and put him to other dreadful barbarities until he died in the greatest agony.

A much gentler valley physically than Cragg Vale is Luddenden Dean, whose biggest settlement in Luddenden. This valley runs from high on Midgley Moor to Luddenden Foot and is perhaps the most beautiful as well as the most interesting of all the small valleys. From the high road near Wainstalls one looks down upon almost the entire length of the valley; Booth, the small village towards the head of it, is perched on a spur of land, while straddling the main road are the impressive works of John Murgatroyd & Son, now closed. The valley is well wooded throughout and steep-sided in its lower reaches. Joining it from Wainstalls one walks down the steep road following the Caty Well Brook, itself wooded and having two dams. On the right is the hamlet of Saltonstall with its attractive seventeenth-century houses and the pub, 'Cat i th' Well', a name meaning nothing more sinister than 'St Catherine's Well'. In the wooded area there are attractive paths on which to wander and a wide open space, a field belonging to Jerusalem Farm, which is used extensively for camping. Higher up, the valley flattens out and there are farms dotted about at either side of Luddenden Brook which in past times formed a township boundary. The fields slope gently on either side of the stream; it is a pastoral valley and at its head are the woods of the Castle Carr Estate. Luddenden Dean has not had the through traffic that some of the other smaller valleys have had, which accounts for the fact that there is no major road out of the head of the valley.

Different again is Hebden Dale, a steep and masculine valley, so steep that it is known as 'Little Switzerland' and containing the famous Hardcastle Crags. One can approach this rugged, thickly wooded valley from several directions: from Nutclough through Midgehole and along the carriage drive to Gibson Mill, itself a superb example of a water-powered textile mill, from Slack Top down the steep rocky sides, or from Pecket Well down the gentle packhorse track. From Crimsworth Dean one can follow the contour round to Walshaw and eventually to the head of the valley, which is markedly different from the green pastoral gentleness of Luddenden Dean. Blake Dean, or Black Dean as it used to be known, is a moorland valley with a stream snaking its way in the bottom. The valley head forms a col from which the road, which runs along the side of the valley, climbs steeply to flatten out again later. Blake Dean is an ideal spot, open, as the thick woods have been left behind, with a green sward at each side of the river, a side valley with a smaller stream and rocks and trees; and it is a popular picnicking spot on summer weekends.

Coming from Queensbury to Halifax, one can look down the full length of Shibden Dale, a magnificent valley. It is quite different in character from any of the other small valleys, being broad and U-shaped, and is divided into a patchwork of green fields dotted with small trees with here and there a house. But it lacks the thick woods of the other valleys. It is, as yet, quite unspoilt, such development as has taken place being on the hilltops which enclose the valley like a horseshoe.

Away from the steep cragginess of the western Pennine valleys, the more gentle rolling countryside of the eastern hill fringes also have their valleys, two of which lie in the rural oasis between Bradford and Leeds, with Pudsey a near neighbour. One is Cockersdale, almost surrounded by an urban skyline and running between two busy main roads. It is a delightfully gentle valley, well wooded with a stream flowing through it and pastoral land on either side. Recently restored by conservation volunteers, it now forms part of the Leeds Country Way. The other valley is the Fulneck Valley, likewise narrow and wooded with a stream from which the surrounding land rises gently.

The two valleys are fringed by very interesting villages. Tong separates them on a ridge of land, hence the derivation of its name, meaning spit of land. It is a charming, rural and unspoilt village. Dr Whitaker described it thus: 'In the midst of manufactures it has preserved its aristocratical character from the earliest times to the present',[2] while a later writer of more than a century ago wrote: '. . . there is a rural aspect about the village of Tong which is truly refreshing to a townsman palled with interminable miles of streets.'[3]

At one end is the hall built by Sir George Tempest in 1702 and now used by a firm of accountants. It is set back from the road along a tree-lined drive and is an attractive building, a squaresashed Italian house, three storeys high, of brick, and one of the first of its type to be introduced into Yorkshire. Next to the hall is the church, a plain structure with, outside the gate, a mounting-block at one side and stocks at the other. The village itself consists of attractive and well-built farmhouses and cottages along the street, with the village pump and pinfold well preserved. ·

Across the valley on a parallel ridge stands the village of Fulneck, described by Dr Whitaker as a long, protracted line of buildings which cannot be said to contribute to the beauties of Tong, though it certainly does not detract from them. The buildings seem to stand in the position of guardian to the gentle beauty of the valley they overlook.

Fulneck was originally 'Fall-neck' – 'neck of land by the clearing'. In 1744 the estate was bought by immigrants whose place of origin was Fulneck in Moravia and who renamed it after their home. The settlement is still there, and the boarding and day schools for boys and girls established by the Moravian Brethren are still flourishing.

A packhorse track connects Fulneck with Tong and goes across into Cockersdale. At one time there was in Tong a blacksmith's shop owned by a family named Oddy whose connection with it covered a span probably of about a couple of centuries. One of them, John Oddy, in the eighteenth century, shod the packhorses which carried bread in panniers from the bakehouse at Fulneck to Gomersal and Wyke. In order to do this he had to be at Fulneck by 4 a.m., carrying sixteen shoes ready sharpened as well as his tools, and he had to take a set of shoes back with him to re-sharpen.

It is logical that an area of dales must also have summits; indeed the public house on the county boundary between West Yorkshire and Greater Manchester is called 'Summit'. West Yorkshire lost its more spectacular summits to North Yorkshire in 1974, the three Peaks of Ingleborough, Penyghent and Whernside, along with Buckden Pike, Great Whernside, Simons Seat and Beamsley Beacon.

Near Todmorden is Studley, marked thus on Jeffery's map of 1775, the name meaning a clearing used as a stud – the local broad pronunciation of the vowel U has corrupted this to 'Stoodley'. Stoodley Pike is the name of the pointed hill overlooking the Calder Valley; the stone man which crowns it and makes it more prominent is not, as is sometimes thought, the Pike. This monument, which itself has had an interesting history, is visible from many miles away. One can, on a clear day, see it from Queensbury and from a long way in the other direction. 'We must be thankful for it,' one woman remarked, 'or else we should have nowhere to walk to.'

There are various ways of getting to the top of Stoodley Pike. The shortest, sharpest and quickest is from Spring Side, up the steep twisting road through the woods to the Stansfield Hospital and then either along the road and up the steep face of the hill or straight up the moorland path from the hospital. A popular way is from the village of Lumbutts or from Mankinholes, where there is a youth hostel. From this end a packhorse track snakes across the fell to the saddle of the moor and then over to Cragg Vale. Once at the saddle there is a large stone post and, marking the way across the barren grassy moorland, smaller posts to guide travellers in misty weather. This is the Pennine Way, and during the summer months one can see many modern two-legged packhorses puffing along the track. For them too the moorland saddle has a guide post, a direction board showing the Pennine Way and the Calderdale Way. One can also approach Stoodley Pike from Cragg Vale, either up the packhorse track from the head of the valley or by way of one of the several tracks which lead from the lower part of it.

One of the most attractive approaches is from Hebden Bridge, where one climbs the steep road to Horse Hold and continues along a grassy packhorse way through Callis Woods out eventually onto another bridle track – that running at the foot of the escarpment of which Stoodley Pike forms part, and going between Mankinholes and Hebden Bridge. This way one approaches the summit very gradually.

The stone monument was built not as a war memorial but as a monument to peace, the first 'man' being erected in 1814 to celebrate the end of the Napoleonic Wars. It was, however, somewhat premature as Napoleon was not finally defeated until the Battle of Waterloo in 1815. The completed monument had a square base and conical tower rising to 113 feet 4 inches. It was weakened by being struck by lightning, eventually collapsing in February 1854, on the day the Russian Ambassador left England prior to the outbreak of the Crimean War. The present 'man' was put up in 1856 and stands 120 feet high, having cost £812 to build, most of the money being raised by public subscription. There is an observation platform forty feet from the ground which is reached by a flight of steps inside the monument. It is wise before embarking on the climb of thirty-nine steps to make sure that there are no previous four-legged visitors. Sheep are easily startled, and it is more than a little disconcerting to be met, in the dark, by several solid four-legged bodies hurtling down. The sheep on Stoodley Pike are extremely matey and come snuffling round expecting to be provided with a free lunch. Enticing though the prospect is, after a long walk, of eating at the summit, it is more prudent to wait until one has walked a little further on the path where there are other outcrops of rock where one can sit, and just below the saddle there is a seat put there in memory of Arthur Archer, the one-time warden of Mankinholes Youth Hostel, where one can sit comfortably.

From the summit the hill curves in a horseshoe formation, the path along the ridge continues over it and into Walsden or round the bottom of it to a pub named, appropriately enough, 'The Shepherd's Rest', from which there is a footpath down into Todmorden. Or one can, from the saddle, drop into Mankinholes and hence into the Calder Valley, or go over into Cragg Vale. But whichever route one selects, the views are incomparable.

One of the facets of modern life is the practice of employing as vehicles of description words which have no bearing whatsoever on the matter in hand; so evolves 'It must have cost a bomb.' This misuse of the language is sufficiently widespread for everyone to know what is meant by such a phrase probably more accurately than if the correct description had been used. As a method of describing the indescribable, it is entirely successful. A man I met once on the saddle above Mankinholes described the country as 'belting'. I knew just what he meant, and it is. So how does one describe the indescribable?

From Stoodley Pike one looks down on Todmorden and right up the deep cleft of the Cliviger Valley. Across, directly in front, the hillside at the other side of the main Calder Valley is rolling and smooth with its patchwork of green fields and black walls punctuated by patches of trees and farm buildings dotted about. Looking in the other direction, one can see right down the valley towards Halifax. This scene is one which can be repeated over and over again in West Yorkshire; one gets so high above the valleys that industry disappears from view. This is especially so in the Huddersfield and Halifax areas, where the rolling hills and the greenness of the area give an impression of the rural heartland of England.

Another famous summit is that of Castle Hill, Almondbury, from which there are splendid views of the distrct. The notion of building a tower – Victoria Prospect Tower – originated as early as 1849, and a private company was formed with this in view. The intention was to build an eight-foot tower and also to have a museum and refreshment rooms, to fill a need for a tourist attraction to the Huddersfield area and more particularly to the village of Almondbury. The scheme came to naught when the agent for the Ramsden estate objected to it. However, the idea was revived on the occasion of Queen Victoria's Diamond Jubilee and the tower was officially opened in June 1899. Stone for it came from Crosland Hill, the wall were built four feet thick at the base and two feet thick at the turret. The tower was not, however, built without some opposition, particularly from people who thought that some more useful memorial, such as a public library, would have been more appropriate.

Other viewpoints are accessible only to walkers. One such summit, although it is really a plateau, is Ilkley Moor, where, 'baht 'at', hundreds, possibly thousands, used to tramp on Bank Holidays. Increasing affluence and the spread of private transport have led people further afield in pursuit of more sophisticated pleasure, but on fine Sundays and Bank Holidays there is still a fair muster. Thirst can be slaked at 'Dick Hudson's' after climbing the hill from Eldwick for the buses were discontinued some years ago; and then one stumbles up the short, narrow, rocky path onto the moor itself.

The path to Ilkley is distinct and well used, so well used that it is almost eroded. Once on top – and the climb from 'Dick's' is scarcely a climb at all – the going is easy. Turning round and looking back, one can see the Aire Valley below, the mills and houses on the edge on Bingley straight in front, to the left the town of Shipley and further left the chimneys and tall buildings of Bradford with the houses creeping further and further up the hillside. The path is sandy with a base of soft gritstone, flanked on either side by heather, and before having gone very far, one is out of sight of all human habitation. Some distance further on, the path descends and divides, crossing rough grass and boggy ground; the two paths eventually unite – one in any case was only a deviation to avoid boggy ground, but now in wet weather the routes are equally boggy.

Following the main path, one can see a glorious view of Wharfedale with the river in the bottom. Immediately below is the clustered town of Ilkley, beyond and to the right a distinctive outcrop of gritstone rock – Almscliff Crag. If one bears right from the main path, eventually the Cow and Calf rocks are reached. These are two enormous boulders which are used by climbers of varying degrees of skill; there is a natural amphitheatre which provides an arena for spectators, for hot-dog stalls and ice-cream caravans and, in times not long past, for Ramblers' Protest Rallies to obtain access to mountains and moorlands.

The entire watershed between the mid Aire and Wharfe is known as Rombalds Moor, a corruption of Romillé after Robert de Romillé to whom Skipton Castle and the neighbouring moors were given after the Norman Conquest. Visible from the Brad-ford, Bingley, Keighley part of the valley is a steep escarpment which stands on the skyline as if someone has sliced off part of the hill with a sharp knife. This is Rivock Edge.

A pleasanter crossing of the moor than the popular one is that going via Doubler Stones and Windgate Nick – local pronunci-ation 'Winyat'. Skirting the base of Rivock Edge, this track crosses rough grass moorland and agricultural land, through a farm, until it reaches two outcrops of Millstone Grit rock with visible marks of wind weathering. These, standing on the edge of heather moorland, are the Doubler Stones. One crosses another stretch of heather moor and suddenly, through a cleft in the escarpment, there is a panoramic view. The view and the suddenness of its appearance are breathtaking. In the immedi-ate foreground is the path snaking through rough moorland which eventually yields to green agricultural land with farms dotted here and there. Beyond in the middle distance is Addingham and in the far distance the fields of lower Wharfedale backed by the hills, the conical regularity of Beamsley Beacon and, beyond, the rocky summit of Simon's Seat.

But the summits are not solely for walkers nor even for car-owners; there are many attractive bus rides over high roads. They do not all, one must hasten to add, get high enough to avoid sight of industry in the valley. Several road summits spring to mind: the high road between Bradford and Bingley through Allerton, Sandy Lane and Walsden, with its views of Airedale; almost the entire bus journey from Bradford to Halifax via Queensbury, where on the Bradford side there are splendid views of Clayton and on the other side impressive views of Halifax and the surrounding moorland. One can go on – there is the road over Cockhill between Oxenhope and Hebden Bridge giving superb views of Crimsworth Dean, and the Stoodley Pike Range; between Halifax and Keighley giving magnificent views of Airedale from Denholme; between Leeds and Otley with glorious views of Lower Wharfedale; the Holme Valley from Holme and the Colne Valley from the hill above Marsden. And away from the high Pennines there is an impressive view from Sandal Castle and an even more impressive one from Woolley Edge. One of the most rewarding sights, on these routes, particularly the more urban ones, appears at night, when the lines of lights along the valleys sparkle like jewelled necklaces.

The moorlands, some with tiny rushing streams and stone clapper bridges over which people walk, are friendly and welcoming; over their paths generations have tramped. During the past hundred years or so, the high, bleak, inhospitable and, in places, dangerous stretches of moorland have 'earned their keep'. For these boggy places are ideal as catchment areas, their soil having natural propensities for water-retention and their surfaces scarred by many small rivulets. Expanding industry and growing towns needed water, and so reservoirs were constructed.

Many of these lie on rambling routes, or perhaps more accurately ramblers use the access roads to the reservoirs. The series at the head of the Colne Valley, the Wessenden group, lying like watery fingers in a deep cleft of moorland, are sombre and uninviting, and yet the track by the side of them and across them provides a satisfying walk. Digley, at the head of the Holme Valley, is bleak but the others in the group, where there are more trees, are rather more exciting. Some, such as the Wessenden group, Booth Wood and Baitings, for example, occupy deep valleys; others, such as Blackstone Edge, White Holme and Warland on Todmorden moor, and the Gorple group, are on a plateau.

Some of the reservoirs are less forbidding, and others lie in less intimidating countryside, such as Eccup; although it is impossible to get right to the edge, one approaches it from an interesting and gentle walk across Alwoodley golf course and through fields, and it is situated in rolling gentle country. Wintersett, a glorious sight when the boats are in full sail, lies in pleasant wooded country, and Scammonden is quite dramatic in its deep valley with the traffic on the M62 roaring past. Ogden lies in wooded country, while Widdop with its arc of gritstone rocks is perhaps the one having the most natural aspect.

11

Tourism

West Yorkshire's moors and summits are, and have been for generations, very precious: 'And the moors were always there, and the horizon never without its promise. No Bruddersford man could be exiled from the uplands and blue air; he always had one foot on the heather, he had only to pay his tuppence on the tram and then climb for half an hour, to hear the larks and curlews, to feel the old rocks warming in the sun, to see the harebells trembling in the shade.'[1] So wrote J. B. Priestley in *Bright Day*; Bruddersford was, of course, Bradford, and although much has changed since the book was published, the core of what Priestley said is still true. The trams have been replaced by buses, and the tuppenny fare has increased somewhat, but it is still possible, just as easily, to reach the moors to which the passage refers. Just how much the modern Bradfordian values the uplands and blue air of his native county is questionable. It is a fair bet that, if there was a threat of its being taken away from him for ever, he would fight for it. But he now seeks his pleasures away from the local moors; increasing affluence and the spread of the motor car have enabled him to enjoy the heather and blue air on more distant moors, and for his annual holiday he can afford to bask in the Mediterranean sun.

The moors to which the passage referred were Shipley Glen and Ilkley Moor. It was a common sight to see, on fine summer Sundays and on Bank Holidays, crowds of people streaming down Victoria Road, across the bridge and the field and up to the Glen. A walk across the Glen brought them to Eldwick and from there up the hill to the Fleece Inn, or alternatively across the fields and along the top road to the Fleece. The inn's most famous landlord in Victorian times was Dick Hudson, who provided teas and was noted for his delicious pies. People used to talk of Dick Hudson's pies and of going to Dick Hudson's, and in time this name for his inn became more famous than the correct one. The name is still in use, and for every hundred people questioned, there is little doubt that ninety-odd per cent would know exactly where 'Dick Hudson's' was, but perhaps only five per cent would know it by its correct name.

The name 'Glen' really refers to the narrow woodland valley with its steep sides and huge Millstone Grit boulders which is flanked by a plateau of moorland, but in common parlance it has come to include the whole area between the Coach Road and the edge of Baildon Moor.

The moor, with its patches of bilberry, rough tussocky grass and outcrops of Millstone Grit, is an ideal area for picnicking and, with the Glen itself nearby, superb for children to play. Beyond in the near distance the vast conurbation of Bradford sprawls, with the chimney of Lister's mill towering over the entire scene.

To the younger end of Bruddersford, the Glen was more important as a playground than as a route to the moors. It was bliss indeed if, in the long school holidays, one's mother, or some one else's, could spare half a day for a trip to Shipley Glen. In a state of great excitement, one skipped down Victoria Road sick with apprehension lest the Glen Tramway would not be open and one would have to walk. Not that the walk was at all arduous but a ride on the tramway was part of the outing, indeed the most important part of the outing. Better fairs than that at the Glen came periodically to the field behind the 'Brown Cow' but nowhere in the vicinity, nowhere anywhere, was there another Glen Tramway. And if the fair was open? How many rides could one afford? Would the man with the punt be there in the Japanese gardens? But no, that was for the tinies. The aerial railway – would one have the nerve to swing along suspended in space? All right if you didn't look down! Perhaps a penny ice-cream would be a better investment. Until . . . here we were and the tramway *was* open.

Towards the end of the nineteenth century Shipley Glen was owned by a Colonel Maude, and it was he who first developed the area to cater for visitors. In the 1890s a Japanese garden was built, containing among other attractions a small boating-pool with a punt propelled by a boatman and a pole. There was also an aerial railway and, certainly later, some swing boats, a roundabout or two, various ice-cream stalls and a café where one could get tea. In 1900 the whole of Shipley Glen was bought by Bradford Corporation.

From Saltaire, in the valley, the moorland part of the Glen rises steeply and can be reached by a footpath. In the 1890s a man named Sam Wilson wished to buy land in order to build a railway from the bottom of Victoria Road to the top of Baildon Moor. With this in view, he asked Sir James Roberts, who was then the owner of Salts Mill, if he would sell him the land. Mr Roberts refused and so Sam Wilson instead bought land from Colonel Maude and on it, in partnership with a Mr Wilkinson, built a cable-hauled tramway which opened in 1895.

Six open toast-rack cars had been used in the Saltaire Exhibition of 1887, and it was these which Sam Wilson bought for his tramway up the Glen. It ran on a double track which was laid to a gauge of one foot eight inches; the maximum gradient was one in twelve and the length 386 yards. The original cars were four toastrack-type trams three feet wide and fourteen feet long, permanently coupled in pairs, and seating was for twelve people on each car. The two pairs of cars were attached to an endless haulage cable powered by a gas engine of eight horsepower. The original cost of the tramway was £998. In 1912 seating accommodation was extended and the cars were able to carry twenty-one people per car. The tramway operated daily from Easter to October, and it is thought that as many as seventeen thousand people have been carried in one day. In 1928 an electric motor was installed to power the winding drum. In 1955 the original cars were withdrawn, and new ones were delivered in 1956 in time for the new season.

The last cars ran at Easter 1981, and the lease was surrendered towards the end of the year. Vandalism occurred but happily the Bradford Trolleybus Society have worked tremendously hard to restore the track, the sheds at the top and bottom and the cars, and the tramway now is in full operation, to the delight of children of all ages. Fares, like everything else, have been subject to inflation. From 1895 to 1951 they remained

static, 1d. up and ½d. down, but they have gradually crept up so
that now they are 15p. up and 10p. down with a 20p return – and
well worth it.

Shipley Glen is still popular: high prices and hard times seem
to be encouraging people to seek pleasures near at hand. The
Japanese gardens have disappeared but the fairground is thriving with its row, its colour and its crowds. There are the aerial
railway, roundabouts and swingboats galore, and for those
whose taste is not pleasure of this nature there is the challenge
of moorland walking and scrambling about in the Glen.

For those citizens of Bruddersford with a little more than
tuppence to spend, there were other moors to explore. For, with
only a little more time, effort and expense, it was possible to get
to Haworth. Situated on the spur of a hill overlooking the Worth
Valley, with its blackened church tower against the sky,
Haworth must be one of the ugliest villages in the county. And
beyond the village the moors have a stark, depressing quality.
Nevertheless, there is some good walking to be had. The route
along the stream from behind the village and up to Top Withens,
associated with 'Wuthering Heights', and down again through
Ponden and Stanbury, is an attractive round walk without
being too strenuous.

Haworth has grown from being an obscure textile village to a
tourist centre drawing crowds of considerable magnitude. The
cause of this is its connection of the Brontës. Lovers of their
books come to see the church where their father was rector, the
parsonage and the museum containing memorabilia as well as
the moorlands which featured in their work. The plethora of
gift, craft, tea and antique shops cater to some degree for the
seething multitudes. One can always rely on the shops in
Haworth being open on a Bank Holiday if one has forgotten a
necessary item.

Crowds come to Haworth by road, by both private and public
transport, and also by rail, the rail link in the valley having had
an interesting history. It was not until the 1860s that a line had
opened up the Worth Valley. The ritual of cutting the first sod,
prior to the construction of the line, was performed on Shrove
Tuesday, 9 February 1864, when at 2 p.m. a procession consisting of anybody who was of any consequence in the neighbour-

hood left the mechanics' institute in Haworth. A spade of carved and polished oak and a handsome polished oak wheelbarrow, both with presentation inscriptions, lent dignity to the sod-cutting ceremony. Later in the afternoon a dinner was held in the National School, the landlord of the 'Black Bull' having done the catering. Difficulty and delay, however, met the promoters of the line after this euphoric start. Although pleas had been made, in the public interest, to landowners along the route to sell land as cheaply as possible, some had cost £80 an acre and some as much as £100 and there were delays in the contractor's getting possession of it. A greater difficulty was one of drainage at Ingrow, where it was necessary to tunnel through the land to take the line under the road. The complexity of this operation threatened the foundations of the Methodist chapel, whose foundation stone had been laid only the previous year by Sir Isaac Holden, chairman of the railway company. It was, as a result, found necessary to build a new chapel, and negotiations about compensation from the railway company dragged on for over four years, eventually going to arbitration, when the trustees were awarded damages of £1,980.

As if these setbacks were not great enough, storms damaged the embankment shortly before the company was about to open the line to traffic. Ill luck was followed by still more ill luck. A date in April 1867 was chosen for the official opening but the train stuck on a gradient part way along the line. A second attempt was made, which attracted no attention in Keighley but was met higher up the line by excited crowds. This train stuck on the damp rails and had to be divided into two sections which were taken to Haworth separately.

There was even a hitch in the arrangements for the celebration dinner, when at short notice it was necessary to transfer it from the 'Black Bull' to the mechanics' institute at Haworth.

The line operated for nearly a century, carrying workers and shoppers and, after the formation of the Brontë Society and the opening of the Brontë Museum at Haworth, increasing numbers of tourists. However, British Rail decided that, in common with many other lines throughout the country, it was to close. In 1961 it closed to passenger traffic, and in 1962 to freight.

The services are now run by the Keighley and Worth Valley

Light Railway, which operates under the auspices of the Keighley and Worth Valley Railway Preservation Society. This, a tourist attraction in itself, provides popular outings for enthusiasts of all ages, as many of the trains are hauled by steam locomotives. The society shares Keighley station with British Rail and from it operates trains right up the valley as far as Oxenhope. The train goes through several interesting stations: Damems was, in the British Rail days, the smallest full-time station on the rail system, and Oakworth, which featured in the film *The Railway Children*, has the distinction of having been voted the best-preserved station in Britain.

At Haworth station there is a working engine shed, and it is often possible to see locomotives which are being prepared for the day's work as well as other engines in various stages of restoration. At Oxenhope station there is an interesting exhibition shed which contains many steam locomotives, vintage carriages and relics of the railway steam age. It is near Oxenhope that the house 'Three Chimneys', which featured in the film *The Railway Children*, is situated. Oxenhope is a pleasant village, in moorland country, and is much quieter and infinitely more attractive than Haworth.

Tourism of a nature similar to that in Haworth has developed in another Pennine village; this is Holmfirth, which is the location for the television series *The Last of the Summer Wine*. Situated in the Holme Valley, Holmfirth grew as a textile centre and is now visited by coachloads of people who come from all parts of the country in order to see in context the buildings which have been immortalized in the television series.

Ancient monuments, like literary shrines, are tourist attractions. A century ago an article was written in which the author spoke sadly of the ravages of time and thoughtless visitors at Sandal Castle. Year by year, he said rather wistfully, the remains of the castle grew less and less. This he blamed on the ruthless hand of time which made no distinction but crumbled ancient monuments to dust, and on stormy winds and rains which beat against the walls in full force. As much to blame were the over-zealous admirers who broke small pieces of stone off the old walls and took them away as articles of curiosity. His article was written at a time when Sandal was a village quite separate from Wakefield – unlike the present, when it is joined by houses into a continuous conurbation – and when the environs were quite rural. The ruins, he said, were approached from the rather romantic Cock and Bottle Lane, so called because it had a public house called the 'Cock and Bottle'. The lane, now, is no longer a lane but a well-maintained road through a housing estate.

His rather pathetic statement that no one seemed willing to restore the fabric is not now true, as Wakefield City Council has done a splendid job, after extensive archaeological research, of restoring and maintaining the site. A substantial path has been constructed right round the motte, and seats have been positioned to enable people to enjoy the view in comfort. There is also a small car-park and adequate facilities for disposing of litter.

With the decline of the traditional industries, efforts have been made and are being made by the County Council and the individual Metropolitan authorities, both separately and in conjunction with private groups and amenity bodies, to develop a tourist industry. It is interesting that a county which has for hundreds of years lived, moved and had its being by wool should build the foundations of its newest industry, tourism, on the textile industry. The latter's physical remains and the transport system it called into being are the basis of much of the new tourism.

Bradford, for instance, has Heritage weekends in which tours are made to the best of the industrial past, including visits to the industrial museum, Salts Mill, Manningham Mills and the model village at Saltaire.

It was common during the 1930s for Sunday School outings and women's meetings on their summer excursion to have half-day trips in scrubbed-out coal barges on the Leeds and Liverpool Canal. A picnic tea would be taken and eaten on Farnhill Moor. Progress was slow and much of the time was taken up with the journey there and back.

During the last decade canals generally have acquired a new lease of life, and canal travel has become popular. There are several canal-cruising companies which hire out craft for private holidays and who also themselves operate cruises. The West Yorkshire Passenger Transport Executive in conjunction

with a cruising company also organizes short canal-boat trips.
There is a through network from the Dewsbury canal basin into
the Leeds and Liverpool Canal. The two sets of locks at
Bingley, the three-rise and the five-rise, provide an interesting
challenge to the cruisers and a never-failing source of entertainment for local people.

Towpaths along the canals make interesting walking ground.
One particularly attractive stretch is that at Marsden at the
head of the Colne Valley, from which it is possible to walk all the
way into Huddersfield town centre. Another is the stretch
between Walsden and Summit on the Rochdale Canal, and
another that between Bingley and Skipton on the Leeds and
Liverpool. There is a project currently in operation to publicize,
as a piece of industrial archaeology, the Standedge Tunnel, and
information boards have been prepared about its history. Pub-
licity about West Yorkshire's industrial heritage is prolific:
there are town trails, mill trails, canal trails, footpath and
bridleway guides; many of the packhorse ways of the Calder
Valley have been incorporated into the long-distance footpath,
the Calderdale Way.

The countryside has been publicized by the designation of
country parks where people can sit, wander, stroll, feed the
ducks or seriously observe nature by following a nature trail, or
by bird watching. One of these is at St Ives, Bingley, a mansion
house in its own grounds standing high above the Aire Valley
with, from certain parts of the park, glorious views. Another is
North Dean Woods, Halifax, where there is a 2½-mile nature
trail. On Castle Hill, Huddersfield, another country park has
been established, and there are others at Shipley Glen and
Golden Acre Park, Leeds. This last is more an artificial park
than the others, having been planted as a botanical garden.
There are alpines, rare trees and shrubs, heathers and azaleas,
while the lake is a major attraction for bird life.

Those who live in the north of the county generally make
tracks for North Yorkshire or Lower Wharfedale for a day or
half-day motoring or walking. Few would dream of going to the
south part of the county. And yet there is some excellent country
here, not spectacular in the way that Calderdale is, but nevertheless extremely attractive. One of the country parks is situ-

ated at Newmillerdam between Wakefield and Barnsley, not a very promising location between two industrial conurbations, one would think.

As early as the fourteenth century the mill at Newmillerdam was known as 'the new mill' but in 1463 the dam seems to have been built, as the name was changed to 'the new mill on the dam'; this was the mill to which the manorial tenants were obliged to bring their corn to be ground. Fishing was popular there, and in 1313 a number of men were fined for fishing at night and for taking water-wolves (perch).

Fishing is still popular, and in the little bays along the shore one can see fishermen. There is a great deal of bird life and in great variety: swans with cygnets who insistently demand a share of one's lunch and hiss and honk alarmingly if one does not oblige. There are also great crested grebes, mallard, Canada geese and common or garden ducks. There are pleasant walks round the lake and out at the far end of the estate to an extremely interesting walk through rolling arable land as far as the village of Notton.

In the same area another country park has been established at Bretton Park, which has interesting nature trails, a lake and nearby a sculpture park. Bretton Hall, which is situated in the park, is now a college of education, and the sculpture park was born as a result of an idea of one of the college lecturers, who knowing the popularity of the nature trail, conceived the idea of a sculpture trail. During discussion of the idea with the Yorkshire Arts Association, it was discovered that there was literally nowhere in Britain where anything similar existed.

Unfortunately the first exhibition of sculpture, held in 1977, was a few years too late to catch the big leap forward in funding the arts. However, financial support for a sculpture park has been forthcoming from many sources: the Yorkshire Arts Association, West Yorkshire County Council, South Yorkshire County Council, the Gulbenkian Foundation, the Henry Moore Foundation, the Danish Government and the Canadian Government, the last named having provided an artist in residence.

The sculpture park is very popular with visitors and has permanent exhibits including a totem pole, a red cedar log which holds its own with the other trees in the park and excites the interest of children. The park also, from time to time, organizes special exhibitions featuring the work of individual sculptors. Its situation at Bretton is particularly significant as two of the foremost Yorkshire and British sculptors came from very near. Bretton is about six miles from Wakefield, where Barbara Hepworth was born, and also near Castleford, the birthplace of Henry Moore.

The County Council has also, in season, inaugurated several scenic bus routes incorporating some of the most glorious countryside in the county which is not regularly served by scheduled buses. One of these goes from Castleford, Pontefract and Featherstone to West Hardwick (where there is a museum), to Nostell Priory and Wintersett, where the reservoir is an interesting sight, especially when the boats are sailing, then via Ryhill, Sandal, Newmillerdam, Woolley Edge, Bretton Country Park and Bretton Sculpture Park and then to Wakefield, returning in reverse order. One can go for the whole ride or get off at any point, and guided walks are organized or one can get leaflets to plan independent excursions. Another route goes from Huddersfield to Hebden Bridge and vice versa, via Outlane, Pole Moor and Nont Sarah's, past Scammonden Dam and Deanhead, Ringstone reservoir, Barkisland, Ripponden, Blackstone Edge, Cragg Vale and Mytholmroyd to Hebden Bridge.

These Wayfarer projects are included in the cheap fares scheme which is operated by the West Yorkshire Passenger Transport Executive in off-peak hours and are funded by the WYPTE and the Countryside Commission with help, in the case of the Wakefield scheme, from Wakefield Metropolitan Council.

Sources

Chapter 2
1. *A picturesque tour through the principal parts of Yorkshire and Derbyshire*, E. Dayes (1825).

Chapter 3
1, 2. *Tour through Great Britain* (1724, 1748, 1762; many editions, three volumes), Daniel Defoe.
3, 4. Diaries of Cornelius Ashworth, transcribed in *Some Aspects of the Eighteenth Century Woollen and Worsted Trade in Halifax*, Frank Atkinson (1956).
5, 6, 7. *The Letter Books of Joseph Holroyd and Sam Hill*, transcribed and edited by Herbert Heaton (Bankfield Museum Notes, 2nd Series, Vol III, 1914).
8. *A Month in Yorkshire* (various editions, 1858, 1879), Walter White.

Chapter 4
1. *British Canals*, Charles Hadfield (early editions published by John Baker, Phoenix House).
2. As 1 above. 5th edition published 1974 by David & Charles. This edition gives the final cost as some £800,000 and the length as 127¼ miles.
3. *A Home Tour Through the Manufacturing Districts of England in the Summer of 1835*, George Head.

Chapter 5
1. *Tour through Great Britain* (1724, 1748, 1762; many editions, three volumes), Daniel Defoe.
2. *Diary*, ii 65–6, Ralph Thoresby, quoted in *The Yorkshire*

Woollen and Worsted Industries, Herbert Heaton (2nd edition, 1965).
3. *A Home Tour Through the Manufacturing Districts of England in the Summer of 1835*, George Head.

Chapter 6
1. *A Topographical description of Cumberland, Westmorland, Lancashire and parts of the West Riding of Yorkshire*, John Housman (1800).
2. *Topographical and statistical description of the County of York*, G. A. Cooke (1818?).
3. *A picturesque tour through the principal parts of Yorkshire and Derbyshire*, E. Dayes (1825).
4. *Directory of the West Riding of Yorkshire*, E. Baines (1822).
5. *The new British traveller*, G. A. Walpoole (1784).
6. *Journal* 9th June, 1757, John Wesley.
7. *The condition of the working class*, Friedrich Engels (1844).
8. *West Riding sketches*, James Burnley (1875).
9. Quoted in *In praise of Yorkshire*, Eleanor Slingsby (1951).
10. Quoted in *Fortunes made in business*, various authors, Volume III (1884–7).
11, 12. As 3 above.
13, 14. *Tour in Germany, Holland and England, 1826, 1827, 1828*, H.L.H. Prince von Pückler-Muskau, Volume IV (1832).
15, 16, 17, 18. As 8 above.
19, 20. *The history and topography of Bradford*, John James (1841).

Chapter 7
1. *The West Riding of Yorkshire*, Joseph E. Morris (third edition, 1932).
2. *West Riding Sketches*, James Burnley (1875).
3. *The new British traveller*, G. A. Walpoole (1784).
4. *Topographical and statistical description of the County of York*, G. A. Cooke (1818?).

Chapter 8
1. *Topographical Description of Cumberland, Westmorland,*

Lancashire and a part of the West Riding of Yorkshire, J. Housman (1800).

2. *Observations on a Tour through almost the whole of England and a considerable part of Scotland*, C. Dibdin (1802).

3. Quoted in *A Regional History of the Railways of Great Britain*, Volume VIII, South and West Yorkshire, David Joy (1975).

Chapter 9

1. *Lower Wharfeland, The Old City of York and The Ainsty*, E. Bogg (1904).

2. *Histories of Bolton and Bowling*, W. Cudworth (1891).

3. *Tour in Germany, Holland and England, 1826, 1827, 1828*, H.L.H. Prince von Pückler-Muskau, Volume IV (1832).

4. *Tour through the northern counties of England*, R. Warner, Volume I (1802).

5. As 2 above.

Chapter 10

1. *First of the century*, W. H. Scott (1901).

2. Quoted in *Round about Bradford*, William Cudworth (1876).

3. *Round about Bradford*, William Cudworth (1876).

Chapter 11

1. *Bright Day*, J. B. Priestley (1946).

Bibliography

There are few books on the county of West Yorkshire as such. The titles listed, although about Yorkshire, or the West Riding of Yorkshire generally, do contain some information about places in West Yorkshire. There are also books – mostly out of print but available in reference libraries – by nineteenth-century antiquarians and topographers as well as town histories and subject histories, e.g. on roads and railways.

Books

Edmund Bogg, *The Old Kingdom of Elmet, York and the Ainsty District*, 1902

G. Douglas Bolton, *Yorkshire Revealed*, Oliver and Boyd, 1955

A. J. Brown, *Moorland Tramping in West Yorkshire*, Country Life and George Newnes, 1931

J. S. Fletcher, *Nooks and Corners of Yorkshire*, Eveleigh Nash, 1911

Marie Hartley and Joan Ingilby, *Getting to Know Yorkshire*, J. M. Dent, 1964

Arthur Mee, *The King's England – West Riding*, Hodder and Stoughton, 1941

David Pill, *Yorkshire – The West Riding*, Batsford, 1977

Ella Pontefract and Marie Hartley, *Yorkshire Tour*, J. M. Dent, 1939

John Porter, *The Making of the Central Pennines*, Moorland Publishing Company, 1980

Arthur Raistrick, *The West Riding of Yorkshire*, In 'The Making of the English Landscape' series, Hodder and Stoughton, 1970

Booklets and pamphlets

Various authors, *The Huddersfield Canals Towpath Guide*, Huddersfield Canal Society, 1981

Ivan E. Broadhead, *Exploring Leeds*, Tetradon Publications, 1981

Jack Reynolds, *Saltaire*, Bradford Art Galleries and Museums, 1976

John S. Roberts, *Little Germany*, Bradford Art Galleries and Museums, 1977

E. M. Savage, *Stoodley Pike*, Todmorden Antiquarian Society, 1974

J. R. Thackrah, *Ilkley*, a Dalesman mini book, Dalesman Publishing Company, 1977

West Yorkshire – enjoy it the car free way, West Yorkshire Passenger Transport Executive, 1982

The following bodies, besides those listed above, issue guidebooks and town trails in the form of pamphlets and booklets, which may be purchased from tourist information offices in the county: Calder Civic Trust, Holme Valley Civic Society, Metropolitan Borough of Calderdale, Sowerby Bridge Civic Society, Worth Valley Railway Preservation Society, and *Yorkshire Ridings Magazine*.

Index